D1320694

ACKNOWLEDGEMENTS

I wish to express my gratitude to Rob Opie and Wendy Botha at Premier Foods, for the opportunity given to me to use such a versatile product range for creating these exciting recipes and for helping to make this book possible. To my family and friends, for all their support, encouragement and tasting throughout the months of recipe testing. To Annelie and Carol, who assisted with the baking for photo shoots, and to Brandon for his magnificent photography. And lastly but so important, the publishing team: Linda de Villiers, for believing so strongly in the Snowflake brand, Joy Clack for her utmost patience with editing and Bev Dodd for the beautiful layout.

Many thanks also go to Yellow Door (Tygervalley and Gardens centres) for some beautiful props, to Nettie for painting special plates and to William for the use of his house during photography.

HEILIE PIENAAR, 2002

First published in 2002 by
New Holland Publishers (UK) Ltd
Garfield House
86-88 Edgware Road
London W2 2EA
London • Cape Town • Sydney • Auckland

www.newhollandpublishers.com

Copyright © 2002 in published edition: Struik Publishers
Copyright © 2002 in text: Premier Foods
Copyright © 2002 in photographs: Premier Foods

All rights reserved. No part of this publication may be reproduced, stored in a retrieval system, or transmitted in any form or by any means, electronic, mechanical, photocopying, recording or otherwise, without the prior written permission of the publishers and copyright holders.

2 3 4 5 6 7 8 9 10

PUBLISHING MANAGER: Linda de Villiers
RECIPE DEVELOPER: Heilie Pienaar
EDITOR: Joy Clack
DESIGNER: Beverley Dodd
COVER DESIGNER: Sean Robertson
PHOTOGRAPHER: Brandon Amron-Coetzee
STYLIST: Heilie Pienaar

Reproduction by Hirt & Carter Cape (Pty) Ltd
Printed and bound by Times Offset (M) Sdn Bhd

ISBN 1 84330 323 X

EGGS: Because of the slight risk of salmonella, raw eggs should not be served to the very young, the ill or elderly or to pregnant woman.

ROYAL ICING (PAGE 106): use a dried egg white substitute.
MARZIPAN (PAGE 106): if you are concerned about the raw egg content in this recipe, use a ready-made marzipan.

CONTENTS

INTRODUCTION

This book is mainly about traditional baking. The basic recipes for scones, cakes, breads, muffins and so on are here, but are sometimes presented in a novel way. Admittedly, some of the recipes are not low in fat, but then again, we are all allowed to enjoy something sweet now and again.

INGREDIENTS

All ingredients should be at room temperature, unless otherwise stated.

Flour

Flour, milled from bread wheats, is the major ingredient used in most baking. It must be of an adequate protein (gluten) strength to:
- form an elastic, extensible dough;
- withstand mixing, stretching and shaping;
- support the weight of other ingredients.

Wheat grain comprises three main parts.
- The bran coating is 14–15% and contains a high proportion of fibre, which aids digestion and prevents constipation. This outer shell is removed to produce white flour.
- The endosperm (inner part of the kernel) is 80–84%. It consists of protein and starch, which are important for energy. White flour is milled from the endosperm.
- The germ is 2–3%. It is present in wholemeal flour, and is milled separately to produce wheatgerm.

Strong or bread flour provides the vital protein needed for bread and pizza doughs. It is the protein that forms gluten when the flour is mixed with liquid to make a dough; the gluten becomes elastic and traps the carbon dioxide gas released as the dough ferments. This causes the dough to rise. If a lighter end product with a softer crumb is desired, a cake for example, a 'softer' flour, lower in protein content, should be used.

Storing

White flours can be stored for up to eight months in cool conditions, or up to a year in a refrigerator or freezer. Bran and wholemeal and brown flours, which can become rancid due to their high bran content, should only be stored for up to three months. Note the following to ensure that flour is maintained in optimum condition:
- Store in an airtight container in a cool, dry place, away from products with strong flavours or odours.
- Do not add fresh flour to old when refilling containers.
- Place a bay leaf in the flour to discourage insect infestation.
- Take note of the 'best before' date stamped on the packet.
- The age of flour, and thus its moisture content, will determine the amount of liquid to be used. The fresher the flour, the less liquid is required. Humidity in the environment will also have an effect. Add liquid gradually, not all at once.

Types of flour

There's a wide variety of flours available for cooking and baking, and getting to know the characteristics of each flour will help to ensure you use the right one for the purpose.

Broadly speaking, flours are defined by the quantities of the wheats used and their rate of extraction. The extraction is the percentage of whole, cleaned wheatgrain in the flour. There are three basic flour categories:
- wholemeal, with 100% extraction, made from the whole wheatgrain with nothing added and nothing taken away;
- brown, with about 85% extraction, as some bran and germ are removed;
- white, usually with 75% extraction, as most of the bran and germ are removed during milling.

Stoneground flour is wholemeal flour ground in a traditional way between two stones, rather than using modern factory rollers. It is usually coarser and heavier than factory-milled flour and is more nutritious as it retains more B vitamins.

Organic flours are milled from grain grown without artificial fertilizers or pesticides on organic farms.

Plain flour

Plain flour, which may be white, brown or wholemeal, is the most widely used. It is milled from a variety of hard and soft wheats, and its protein content usually ranges from seven to ten per cent. Plain flour is ideal for cakes, biscuits, most pastries and general cooking, such as coating food and thickening sauces and gravies.

Clockwise from top left: *Wheatgerm flour, Bread flour, Brown bread flour, Wheat bran, Semolina, Plain flour, Self-raising flour.*

Self-raising flour

This is white, brown or wholemeal flour to which a raising agent has been added to give lightness to the baked product. It is usually used for scones, cakes and biscuits, and quick breads or teabreads.

After opening, self-raising flour must be stored in an airtight container to preserve the raising agent. To make your own self-raising flour, add 1 tsp baking powder to each 125 g (4½ oz) plain flour. Always sift this before using to mix it evenly.

Bread flour

Also called strong plain flour, this is usually white although brown and wholemeal bread flours are available. Bread flour has a protein content of 11–14%, which makes it the best flour for yeasted doughs. It is also excellent for making puff pastry.

Granary flour

Also called malted wheatgrain flour, this is brown flour milled from malted wheat (grains that have been allowed to begin fermenting) to which whole and cracked wheatgrains are added. Granary flour has a distinctive nutty flavour and texture.

Wheatgerm flour

This is white or brown flour with at least 10% wheatgerm added to it.

Spelt flour

Milled from an ancient ancestor of wheat, spelt flour is more nutritious, but contains less protein than modern wheat flour.

Semolina

Durum wheat, a 'hard' wheat with a high protein content, is the source of semolina. It is milled to produce the traditional flour for making pasta. Semolina is also used to make gnocchi (small dumplings) and couscous, as well as milk puddings.

Wheat bran

The outer layer of the wheat kernel is removed to produce bran, an unrefined by-product of flour. Wheat bran is rich in hemi-cellulose, fibre, vitamins and minerals and can be added to breads, scones and muesli. It can also be sprinkled over porridge and cereal. Store it for three to four months under ideal conditions, and up to a year in a refrigerator or freezer.

Non-wheat flours

Wheat flour is the most commonly used, but other grains are also milled into flour. These can be blended with wheat flour or used on their own, to give variety to your cooking and baking.

Those that are gluten-free are ideal for people with gluten intolerance.

- barley flour has a sweet nutty flavour; it is low in gluten so not ideal for baking unless mixed with wheat flour;
- buckwheat flour contains no gluten so cannot be used for yeasted doughs. However, it is useful for scones, pancakes and blinis, and flat breads;
- cornmeal or maize meal has a slightly granular texture and is gluten-free; it is cooked to make polenta and is also used for breads and muffins;
- gram or chickpea flour is a gluten-free flour traditionally used for chapattis and other flat breads;
- oat flour and oatmeal are used with wheat flour for all sorts of baking;
- rye flour, low in gluten, gives bread a rich flavour and chewy texture;
- soya flour, milled from raw or toasted soya beans, is high in protein but gluten-free.

Butter

Butter is important for any baking. It gives cakes, biscuits and pastries a rich flavour, tenderness or crispness and a warm subtle colour. Unsalted butter is preferable for cakes and biscuits.

Storing

Chilled, salted butter keeps well for up to one month and unsalted butter for up to two weeks. Butter freezes well for up to six months.

Baking

It is important to use butter at the correct temperature. For biscuits, cakes and breads, use at room temperature for better creaming with sugar.

Alternatives/substitutions

Margarine can be used instead of butter in most recipes, but the creamy taste of butter is necessary for delicate pastries. If substituting margarine, use the hard, block type. The soft type (tub) has a higher water content and should only be used when mentioned specifically.

Sugar

Caster sugar

This is the kind most used in baking. It is ideal for creaming as well as for whisking with eggs as its fine grains dissolve quickly. Caster sugar is also used for meringues.

Granulated sugar

This has larger grains than caster sugar, so if used in delicate cakes it can cause a speckled appearance. It can be used for rubbed-in mixtures such as for biscuits, in place of caster sugar, if preferred.

Icing sugar

Almost powdery in texture, icing sugar dissolves immediately. It is used mainly for smooth icings, but is also excellent for meringues, whipped cream, sifting over pies and desserts and for decorations. Icing sugar is not usually used in cake mixtures as it does not create enough volume when creamed.

Soft brown sugar

Whether light or dark, this is a refined white sugar coloured with syrup or molasses.

SUBSTITUTING INGREDIENTS

230 g (8¼ oz) butter	220 ml (7½ fl oz) sunflower or other mild oil
1 tbsp cornflour	2 tbsp plain flour
125 g (4½ oz) self-raising flour	125 g (4½ oz) plain flour + 1 tsp baking powder
4 tsp baking powder	2 tsp cream of tartar + 1 tsp bicarbonate of soda
1 tsp cream of tartar	1 tbsp lemon juice or vinegar or ½ tsp tartaric acid
1 tbsp easy-blend yeast	25 g (scant 1 oz) fresh yeast
210 g (7½ oz) caster sugar	220 g (8 oz) golden syrup or honey
250 ml (8½ fl oz) soured cream	250 ml (8½ fl oz) milk + 4 tsp lemon juice or 1 tbsp vinegar
250 ml (8½ fl oz) yoghurt	250 ml (8½ fl oz) buttermilk or soured cream
250 ml (8½ fl oz) cream	185 ml (6½ fl oz) milk + 65 g (2¼ oz) butter or 170 ml (scant 6 fl oz) buttermilk + 80 ml (2¾ fl oz) sunflower oil
1 whole egg in biscuits and cakes	2 tbsp water + ½ tsp baking powder or 1 egg white + 2 tsp sunflower oil
1 tsp lemon juice	½ tsp vinegar
30 g (1 oz) chocolate	25 g (scant 1 oz) cocoa + 2 tsp butter

NB: If you can't find a can of the exact weight specified, use the nearest to it.

Demerara sugar

Deep gold in colour, with slightly sticky, large crystals, demerara is an unrefined sugar derived from raw sugar cane.

Muscovado sugar

Soft and fine in texture, this unrefined sugar may be light or dark. It is used when a rich molasses-type flavour is required, such as in gingerbreads or fruit cakes.

Eggs

Eggs are indispensable in baking. They can be used whole or separately as yolks and whites to bind a mixture, to add richness and to create volume. All recipes in this book have been tested using large eggs. It is preferable not to use smaller eggs. The colour of the shell does not determine the flavour, but size makes a difference.

Storing

Bake with fresh eggs. Eggs should not be older than 21 days. Refrigerate with pointed ends facing down.

To test if an egg is fresh, immerse it horizontally in cold water. If it is fresh it will sink to the bottom without tilting. If it tilts, it may be up to a week old. If it floats vertically, it is old.

Baking

Eggs should be at room temperature before baking. If they are too cold the whites won't whisk up to the required volume. When whisking egg whites, ensure that no yolk is present and that the bowl is completely grease-free. Only whisk egg whites just before using as they lose volume quickly. Do not over beat. Egg yolks, on the other hand, will curdle quickly if they are too cold or if added to a cake mixture too quickly. Add beaten egg a little at a time, and sprinkle in a tablespoon of flour if the mixture starts to curdle.

Substituting

Eggs are not easy to substitute. In baking, they provide richness, colour and protein. Most baking problems start when substituting eggs or fats. Egg whites provide extra volume and air. Eggs are also used for binding.

When substituting eggs, it is important to know the purpose they serve in the recipe. If the recipe calls for one egg, it normally serves as a binding agent. More than three eggs cannot be substituted successfully. In some recipes, for example light sponge cakes, only eggs will do.

Baking powder

This is a mixture of bicarbonate of soda, starch and acids, used to make cakes and some light doughs rise. The acids in the baking powder react with the bicarbonate of soda when liquid is added, releasing the carbon dioxide that aerates the mixture.

Bicarbonate of soda

This reacts with acids such as the cream of tartar in baking powder, or buttermilk and yoghurt in a mixture, and releases carbon dioxide. When bicarbonate of soda is used alone, and not as a component of baking powder, the cake, quick bread, scones or other items must be baked immediately. Delays will result in a loss of volume. Too much bicarbonate of soda gives quick breads a soapy flavour with an acid smell. Both bicarbonate of soda and baking powder have a fine texture and do not need to be dissolved in hot water.

Yeast

Easy-blend yeast, also called fast-action yeast, is a dried yeast to which Vitamin C has been added. Easy-blend yeast can be mixed directly with flour. If you prefer to use ordinary dried yeast it must be dissolved in tepid water and then left to stand until frothy before being added to the flour.

TYPES OF PASTRY

Shortcrust pastry

This contains one part fat to two parts flour. Keep ingredients cool, work quickly and chill pastry before rolling out. Shortcrust pastry dishes include single crust pies, savoury flans and quiches, and sweet tarts.

Rich shortcrust pastry

This pastry can be rolled out more thinly than basic shortcrust. Egg yolk and sugar are usually added, resulting in a richer pastry that will stay crisp for longer. This pastry is ideal for tartlet shells and is often baked blind.

Sweet flan pastry

This pastry is similar to rich shortcrust pastry, with the addition of an extra egg, sugar and vanilla essence.

Puff pastry

An equal proportion of fat to flour is usually used to make this pastry. Puff pastry has a texture that is delicate, fine and flaky, and is ideal for making pie toppings, fine pastries and tarts.

Flaky pastry

This is not as delicate as puff pastry, but it is flaky, rises high and can be used for the same purposes.

Cream cheese pastry

This rich pastry, made with cream cheese or sieved cottage cheese, can be used for sweet or savoury dishes. The pastry is easy to handle if the ingredients are cold.

Soda-water pastry

This is a good substitute for puff pastry as it also has a layered appearance. It is ideal for sweet or savoury dishes.

Choux pastry

This pastry differs from all others because it is made in a saucepan, is soft and has to be piped or spooned. Choux pastry should be baked until dry to ensure it holds its shape.

GENERAL BAKING RULES

– Read the recipe carefully. Make sure you have all the ingredients before you start.

– Measure and weigh ingredients accurately.

– Always sift flour to aerate it.

– Unless otherwise specified, use ingredients at room temperature.

– Use either metric or imperial, not a mixture of the two, as they are not exact equivalents.

– The correct baking tin is essential. Measure across the top on the inside of the tin.

METRIC/IMPERIAL CONVERSION TABLES

When preparing recipes in this book, use all metric or all imperial measures as the two sets of measurements are not exact equivalents.

Volume measures

75 ml (2½ fl oz)	240 ml (8 fl oz)	500 ml (17 fl oz)	1.4 litres (2½ pints)
90 ml (3 fl oz)	250 ml (8½ fl oz)	600 ml (1 pint)	1.5 litres (2¾ pints)
100 ml (3½ fl oz)	300 ml (10 fl oz)	750 ml (1¼ pints)	1.7 litres (3 pints)
120 ml (4 fl oz)	360 ml (12 fl oz)	900 ml (1½ pints)	2 litres (3½ pints)
150 ml (5 fl oz)	400 ml (14 fl oz)	1 litre (1¾ pints)	3 litres (5¼ pints)
200 ml (7 fl oz)	450 ml (15 fl oz)	1.2 litres (2 pints)	

Weights

10 g (¼ oz)	115 g (4 oz)	400 g (14 oz)	1.25 kg (2¾ lb)
15 g (½ oz)	125 g (4½ oz)	450 g (1 lb)	1.35 kg (3 lb)
20 g (¾ oz)	140 g (5 oz)	500 g (1 lb 2 oz)	1.5 kg (3 lb 3 oz)
25 g (scant 1 oz)	150 g (5½ oz)	550 g (1¼ lb)	1.8 kg (4 lb)
30 g (1 oz)	170 g (6 oz)	600 g (1 lb 5 oz)	2 kg (4½ lb)
45 g (1½ oz)	200 g (7 oz)	675 g (1½ lb)	2.25 kg (5 lb)
50 g (1¾ oz)	225 g (8 oz)	750 g (1 lb 10 oz)	2.5 kg (5½ lb)
55 g (2 oz)	250 g (8½ oz)	800 g (1¾ lb)	2.7 kg (6 lb)
75 g (2½ oz)	280 g (10 oz)	900 g (2 lb)	3 kg (6½ lb)
85 g (3 oz)	300 g (10½ oz)	1 kg (2¼ lb)	
100 g (2½ oz)	340 g (12 oz)	1.1 kg (2½ lb)	

Linear measures

3 mm (⅛ in)	6 cm (2½ in)	20 cm (8 in)	50 cm (20 in)
5 mm (¼ in)	7.5 cm (3 in)	23 cm (9 in)	61 cm (24 in)
1 cm (½ in)	10 cm (4 in)	25 cm (10 in)	77 cm (30 in)
2 cm (¾ in)	12 cm (5 in)	28 cm (11 in)	
2.5 cm (1 in)	15 cm (6 in)	30 cm (12 in)	
5 cm (2 in)	18 cm (7 in)	46 cm (18 in)	

- As most recipes require a preheated oven, switch on the oven before starting your preparation.
- The baking times given in each recipe are only to be used as a guide. Ovens and bakeware vary and this can affect the final baking times. Changes in ingredients can also affect the baking time.
- Check cakes 5 minutes before the end of the baking time. Use a cake tester to test if cooked through.

KITCHEN EQUIPMENT

The most basic equipment is usually enough, although electric mixers and food processors make baking much easier and quicker. Electronic equipment – digital scales for example – are extremely useful as it is always advisable to measure accurately. Before starting to bake, ensure that you have all the equipment you need.

OVENS

Always allow a minimum of 2.5 cm (1 in) around tins for even heat distribution. When baking on more than one shelf, rearrange the tins halfway through the baking time.

Fan ovens are ideal for baking as a fan circulates the heat inside the oven, resulting in an even temperature throughout. As baking times are often slightly less in a fan oven, adjust the temperature as required.

Microwave ovens

None of these recipes has been tested in a microwave oven as the cooking times and results are very different from baking in a standard oven.

BAKING TRAYS AND TINS

Non-stick coated or heavy-duty aluminium tins are best as this material distributes the heat evenly. Grease tins with a sprayed-on non-stick coating or a brush dipped in melted butter. Lining tins with greaseproof paper or baking parchment is also advised.

For best results, always use the size indicated in a recipe to avoid overflowing. A guideline is to fill tins to no more than half to two-thirds full, thus leaving room for expansion.

CONVERSION TABLE

Teaspoons

scant ½ tsp	2 ml
½ tsp	3 ml
1 tsp	5 ml
2 tsp	10 ml
4 tsp	20 ml

Tablespoons

1 Tbsp	15 ml
2 Tbsp	30 ml
3 Tbsp	45 ml

OVEN TEMPERATURES

	°C	°F	gas mark
very cool	100	200	¼
very cool	120	250	½
cool	150	300	2
moderate	160	325	3
moderate	180	350	4
moderate hot	190	375	5
hot	200	400	6
hot	220	425	7
very hot	240	475	9

TIN SIZES

Measure across the top, on the inside of the tin.

Springform tin, round	23 cm (9 in)
Cake tin	20 cm (8 in)
Loose-bottomed cake tin	23 cm (9 in)
Ring tin	22 cm (8¾ in)
Deep square cake tin	20 cm (8 in)
Loaf tin	23 cm (9 in)
Loose-bottomed tart tin	24 cm (9½ in)
Fluted flan tin	24 cm (9½ in)
Pizza tin	25 cm (10 in)
Square tin	24 cm (9½ in)
Rectangular tin	24 x 34 cm (9½ x 14 in)
Rectangular tin	20 x 24 cm (8 x 9½ in)
Tray bake tin	16 x 26 cm (6½ x 10½ in)
Swiss roll tin	23 x 32 cm (9 x 13 in)

BISCUITS AND RUSKS

BISCUITS

Ingredients

The quality of the ingredients is always important, yet it is not as critical with biscuits as it is with cakes. When baking biscuits, many different variations can be achieved by swapping the flavouring ingredients.

Dropped biscuits

The dough is usually very soft and is spooned onto greased baking trays. Leave enough space between each biscuit to allow room for spreading.

Rolled biscuits

The dough is firm and can therefore be rolled out thinly, to a thickness of 2–3 mm (about 1/8 in), before being cut into shapes with a biscuit cutter. Roll out the dough on a lightly floured surface – don't use too much flour as this will make the dough tough. If the dough is sticky, roll it out between sheets of greaseproof paper. Roll in one direction to produce an even thickness.

Shaped biscuits

The dough is usually soft and is forced through a piping bag fitted with a nozzle. When firmer dough is used it is shaped by hand or pressed through a biscuit maker. It may also be chilled before baking to maintain its shape.

Refrigerator biscuits

The dough is shaped into long sausage forms and is chilled or frozen before being cut into slices with a sharp knife. The slices are then arranged on greased baking trays and baked.

Baking

Leave at least 2.5 cm (1 in) between the baking tray and the sides of the oven. When using a standard oven, ideally bake one tray of biscuits at a time – the best results are achieved using the middle shelf. If baking on more than one baking tray, swap their positions halfway through to achieve more even baking. If you are using a fan oven, more biscuits can be baked at a time because all oven shelves can be used. Biscuits normally bake quickly, 10–15 minutes in total in a moderate oven.

Cooling and storing

Biscuits are normally soft when removed from the oven, but will harden as they cool. The longer they are baked, the harder they will become. Some biscuits bake brittle and need to be removed carefully before being placed on wire racks to cool. Make sure that the biscuits are cold before storing in an airtight container. They must be stored on their own as they soften quickly and can absorb other flavours.

When un-iced biscuits start to soften they can be crisped again by heating in a moderate oven for about 5 minutes. Hard biscuits can be successfully frozen for up to three months, and will defrost within one hour at room temperature.

CHOCOLATE CHUNK BISCUITS

200 g (7 oz) butter or margarine
100 g (3½ oz) caster sugar
65 g (2¼ oz) light brown sugar
2 large eggs
1 tsp vanilla essence
250 g (8½ oz) self-raising flour
150 g (5½ oz) dark chocolate, coarsely chopped

1 Cream the butter and both sugars together. Add eggs and vanilla essence and beat well until light and fluffy.

2 Sift flour and add, mixing well. Stir in chocolate chunks.

3 Drop teaspoonfuls onto a greased baking tray and bake in a preheated oven at 180 °C (350 °F, gas mark 4) for 10–12 minutes.

4 Remove biscuits and place on a wire rack to cool.

MAKES ABOUT 60

VARIATION
Substitute chopped chocolate pieces with chocolate chips.

TIP
To make fine crumbs, place any crispy biscuits inside a plastic bag and use a rolling pin to crush them until fine.

Chocolate Chunk Biscuits

COTTAGE DELIGHTS

450 g (1 lb) butter or margarine
210 g (7½ oz) caster sugar
1 tsp lemon or almond essence
397 g can condensed milk
625 g (1 lb 6 oz) plain flour
4 tsp baking powder
scant ½ tsp salt

1 Cream the butter and sugar. Add the lemon or almond essence and condensed milk and beat well.

2 Sift the remaining ingredients and mix into the butter mixture.

3 Shape teaspoonfuls of dough into balls. Place on greased baking trays and flatten slightly with a fork.

4 Bake in a preheated oven at 160 °C (325 °F, gas mark 3) for 15–20 minutes. Transfer to a wire rack to cool. Store in an airtight container.

MAKES ABOUT 90

TIPS
- Sprinkle a layer of sugar in the bottom of the storage container to keep biscuits or rusks fresh for longer.
- Undecorated biscuits that start going soft can be crisped up in the oven at 180 °C (350 °F, gas mark 4) for 5 minutes.

JAM AND COCONUT COOKIES

250 g (8½ oz) plain flour
2 tsp baking powder
scant ½ tsp salt
2 tbsp + 150 g (5½ oz) caster sugar
125 g (4½ oz) butter or margarine
3 large eggs, separated
3 tbsp water
280 g (10 oz) smooth apricot jam
160 g (5¾ oz) desiccated coconut

1 Sift flour, baking powder and salt. Add 2 tbsp caster sugar. Rub in butter.

2 Add egg yolks and water and knead to a soft dough. Roll out to 3 mm (⅛ in) thick. Stamp out rounds of about 7 cm (scant 3 in) in diameter. Press into greased patty tins. Spoon 2 tsp apricot jam into each.

3 Whisk egg whites until stiff and add remaining caster sugar and coconut. Spoon about 1 tbsp egg white mix over apricot jam.

4 Bake in a preheated oven at 180 °C (350 °F, gas mark 4) for 20–25 minutes. Remove and cool on a wire rack.

MAKES ABOUT 18

VARIATION
Substitute apricot jam with any other flavour jam.

TIP
Sprinkle just enough flour on the work surface and rolling pin to prevent sticking. Excess flour may cause the cookies to be hard.

SHORTBREAD TWIRLS

250 g (8½ oz) butter or margarine
1 tsp vanilla essence
1 tsp almond essence
105 g (3¾ oz) caster sugar
250 g (8½ oz) plain flour
scant ½ tsp salt
1 tbsp milk

1 Cream butter, both essences and sugar together until light and fluffy.

2 Sift flour and salt and add to the mixture, together with the milk.

3 Spoon the mixture into a piping bag fitted with a large star nozzle and pipe decorative shapes onto a greased baking tray.

4 Bake in a preheated oven at 160 °C (325 °F, gas mark 3) for 12–15 minutes, or until lightly browned. Transfer to a wire rack to cool.

MAKES ABOUT 20

VARIATIONS
For chocolate shortbread, omit the milk and add 2 tbsp cocoa powder mixed with 2 tbsp hot water to the shortbread mixture. Mix well.
Alternatively, dip one side of each biscuit into melted chocolate, or drizzle chocolate over the top.

Left to right: *Shortbread Twirls, Jam and Coconut Cookies, Cottage Delights.*

BUTTERSCOTCH BISCUITS

250 g (8½ oz) butter or margarine
300 g (10½ oz) brown sugar
2 large eggs
1 tsp vanilla essence
440 g (15½ oz) plain flour
1 tsp baking powder
½ tsp bicarbonate of soda
200 g (7 oz) walnuts or pecan nuts, chopped

1 Cream butter and sugar. Add eggs, one at a time, and beat until light and fluffy. Add vanilla essence.

2 Sift flour, baking powder and bicarbonate of soda and add. Add nuts.

3 Shape into two rolls of 24 cm (9½ in) in length. Wrap in greaseproof paper and chill or freeze until hard.

4 Slice into biscuits of 1 cm (½ in) in thickness and arrange on greased baking trays. Bake in a preheated oven at 180 °C (350 °F, gas mark 4) for 15–20 minutes until light brown. Transfer to a wire rack to cool.

MAKES ABOUT 50

VARIATION
Make crumbs from these biscuits and use them as a base for a delicious tart. Mix 100 g (3½ oz) melted butter with the crumbs and use as a base for the Ginger and Cherry Flan (page 68).

RICH ALMOND BISCUITS

125 g (4½ oz) plain flour
120 g (4½ oz) cornflour
100 g (3½ oz) ground almonds
52 g (2 oz) caster sugar
scant ½ tsp vanilla essence
scant ½ tsp salt
200 g (7 oz) soft butter or margarine
1 tsp grated lemon rind (optional)
about 3 tbsp icing sugar for rolling

1 Sift flour and mix with all other ingredients except icing sugar. Shape teaspoonfuls of mixture into balls and place on greased baking trays.

2 Bake in a preheated oven at 160 °C (325 °F, gas mark 3) for 30–35 minutes. Leave to cool slightly. Roll in icing sugar.

MAKES ABOUT 48

MELTING MOMENTS

375 g (13 oz) butter or margarine
130 g (4½ oz) icing sugar
350 g (12½ oz) flour
30 g (1 oz) custard powder
pinch of salt

1 Cream butter and icing sugar. Sift flour, custard powder and salt together and add to the butter mixture.

2 Knead well and shape teaspoonfuls of mixture into balls. Place on lightly greased baking trays and bake in a preheated oven at 180 °C (350 °F, gas mark 4) for 15–20 minutes. Transfer to a wire rack to cool.

MAKES ABOUT 50

CRUNCHIES

250 g (8½ oz) plain flour
2 tsp baking powder
2 tsp bicarbonate of soda
scant ½ tsp salt
160 g (5¾ oz) rolled oats
80 g (2¾ oz) desiccated coconut
15 g (½ oz) wheat bran
200 g (7 oz) butter or margarine
300 g (10½ oz) granulated sugar
2 tbsp golden syrup or honey

1 Sift the flour, baking powder, bicarbonate of soda and salt. Add oats, coconut and bran.

2 In a heavy-based saucepan, melt the butter, sugar and syrup and add it to the dry ingredients. Mix well. Press into a 16 x 26 cm (6½ x 10½ in) tray bake tin.

3 Bake in a preheated oven at 180 °C (350 °F, gas mark 4) for 10 minutes. Cool and cut into squares.

MAKES ABOUT 24

VARIATION
Substitute plain flour with brown or granary flour for a crunchy bite.

TIP
If sealed in an airtight container, desiccated coconut freezes well for up to six months.

Clockwise from left: *Rich Almond Biscuits, Butterscotch Biscuits, Ginger Cookies.*

GINGER COOKIES

200 g (7 oz) soft butter or margarine
200 g (7 oz) caster sugar
1 large egg
1 tbsp milk
4 tbsp golden syrup or honey
315 g (10¾ oz) plain flour
1 tbsp ground ginger
1 tsp bicarbonate of soda
½ tsp ground cinnamon
scant ½ tsp salt
2 tbsp granulated sugar for rolling

1 Cream the butter and caster sugar until light and fluffy. Beat in egg, then stir in the milk and syrup.

2 Sift the flour, ginger, bicarbonate of soda, cinnamon and salt together and add to butter mixture. Mix well. Shape the dough into balls and roll them in the granulated sugar.

3 Arrange cookies on greased baking trays, leaving room for spreading, and flatten slightly with a fork.

4 Bake in a preheated oven at 180 °C (350 °F, gas mark 4) for 8–10 minutes. Leave to cool slightly before transferring to a wire rack to cool completely. Store in an airtight container.

MAKES ABOUT 40

TIP
Dip the fork in flour to minimise sticking when flattening out the biscuits on a baking tray.

SURPRISE BITES

125 g (4½ oz) butter or margarine
52 g (2 oz) caster sugar
155 g (5½ oz) plain flour
25 g (scant 1 oz) chocolate chips
50 g (1¾ oz) red glacé cherries,
coarsely chopped

1 Cream butter and sugar well. Sift flour and mix well into butter mixture. Roll out dough to a thickness of 2–3 mm (about ⅛ in). Stamp out with a round biscuit cutter of about 6 cm (2½ in) in diameter.

2 Alternating between the two, place chocolate chips and cherries in the centre of half of the pastry rounds. Top each with a second round of pastry and seal the edges.

3 Bake in a preheated oven at 200 °C (400 °F, gas mark 6) for 8–10 minutes. Transfer to a wire rack to cool.

MAKES ABOUT 15 DOUBLE BISCUITS

VARIATION
To make herb biscuits: substitute chocolate chips and cherries with 4 tbsp chopped fresh mixed herbs, and knead into the dough.

TIPS
- To seal the biscuits, brush a little water or milk onto the edges of the pastry before topping with a second pastry round.
- If you don't have a biscuit cutter, cut out the shapes using a thin-edged glass.

SPICY OAT AND RAISIN COOKIES

200 g (7 oz) soft butter or margarine
150 g (5½ oz) caster sugar
150 g (5½ oz) light brown sugar
2 large eggs
1 tsp vanilla essence
185 g (6½ oz) plain flour
1 tsp bicarbonate of soda
½ tsp ground cinnamon
scant ½ tsp salt
160 g (5¾ oz) rolled oats
150 g (5½ oz) seedless raisins

1 Cream butter and both sugars until well mixed. Beat in eggs, one at a time, until light and fluffy. Add vanilla essence.

2 Sift the flour, bicarbonate of soda, cinnamon and salt together. Gradually beat into butter mixture. Stir in oats and raisins. Drop teaspoonfuls of mixture onto greased baking trays, or shape into balls if preferred.

3 Bake in a preheated oven at 180 °C (350 °F, gas mark 4) for 8–10 minutes or until golden brown. Transfer to a wire rack to cool.

MAKES ABOUT 40

TIP
Allow enough space between cookies on the baking tray as the dough will spread slightly.

TRADITIONAL SHORTBREAD

250 g (8½ oz) butter, softened
105 g (3¾ oz) caster sugar
315 g (10¼ oz) plain flour
60 g (2 oz) cornflour
scant ½ tsp salt
extra caster sugar for sprinkling

1 Beat butter and sugar until light and fluffy. Sift the remaining ingredients and add.

2 Knead lightly and press into a greased 16 x 26 cm (6½ x 10½ in) tray bake tin. Prick very well and bake in a preheated oven at 130 °C (270 °F, gas mark 1) for about 1 hour.

3 Cut into fingers while still hot and sprinkle lightly with extra caster sugar.

MAKES ABOUT 24 FINGERS

VARIATION
For a citrus flavour, add 1 tbsp grated lemon or orange rind.

TIP
Shortbread bakes more evenly when pricked all over with a fork.

Left to right: *Traditional Shortbread, Surprise Bites.*

CHEESY BARBECUE BISCUITS

125 g (4½ oz) plain flour
200 g (7 oz) Cheddar cheese, grated
100 g (3½ oz) butter or margarine
125 g (4½ oz) packet barbecue
flavour crisps, crushed

1 Mix all ingredients together to form a soft dough.

2 Shape teaspoonfuls of dough into balls. Place on greased baking trays and flatten slightly with a fork.

3 Bake in a preheated oven at 200 °C (400 °F, gas mark 6) for about 10 minutes, or until light brown. Transfer to a wire rack to cool. Store these biscuits in an airtight container.

MAKES ABOUT 24

VARIATION
Substitute the crisps with any other flavour of choice, such as cheese and onion.

SPICY BISCUITS

250 g (8½ oz) butter
500 g (1 lb 2 oz) caster sugar
2 large eggs
625 g (1 lb 6 oz) plain flour
4 tsp baking powder
2 tsp mixed spice
4 tsp ground cinnamon
1 tsp ground ginger
½ tsp ground cloves
½ tsp bicarbonate of soda

1 Cream butter and sugar. Add eggs and beat well until light and creamy.

2 Sift remaining ingredients and add to butter mixture, with a little water if required, and bind into a dough.

3 Roll out to a thickness of 2–3 mm (about ⅛ in) and cut out with a biscuit cutter. Place on a greased baking tray and bake in a preheated oven at 180 °C (350 °F, gas mark 4) for 8–10 minutes. Place on a rack to cool.

MAKES ABOUT 55

RICH CHOCOLATE CHIP COOKIES

125 g (4½ oz) butter or margarine
2 tbsp caster sugar
125 ml (4 fl oz) condensed milk
185 g (6½ oz) self-raising flour
80 g (2¾ oz) chocolate chips

1 Cream butter and sugar. Beat in condensed milk, then sift flour and add to mixture with chocolate chips.

2 Roll teaspoonfuls of mixture into balls and place on greased baking trays. Flatten slightly with a fork.

3 Bake in a preheated oven at 160 °C (325 °F, gas mark 3) for 15–20 minutes. Transfer to a wire rack to cool.

MAKES ABOUT 28

TIP
The dough can be made in advance and refrigerated. Bake batches of cookies as required.

MILLIONAIRE'S SHORTBREAD

SHORTBREAD
125 g (4½ oz) butter
105 g (3¾ oz) caster sugar
125 g (4½ oz) plain flour
2 tbsp cornflour
scant ½ tsp salt

FUDGE LAYER
75 g (2½ oz) butter
60 g (2 oz) golden syrup
397 g can condensed milk
105 g (3¾ oz) caster sugar

CHOCOLATE TOPPING
150 g (5½ oz) dark chocolate

1 For shortbread: beat butter and sugar until light and fluffy. Sift flour, cornflour and salt. Mix into butter-sugar mixture until a stiff dough is formed.

2 Press into a greased 20 x 24 cm (8 x 10 in) rectangular tin. Prick with a fork and bake in a preheated oven at 180 °C (350 °F, gas mark 4) for 10 minutes. Reduce heat to 160 °C (325 °F, gas mark 3) and bake for a further 10 minutes.

3 For fudge layer: boil all ingredients in a saucepan for about 5 minutes, until thick. Beat constantly to prevent burning. Spread over baked shortbread and leave to cool until set.

4 For chocolate topping: melt the chocolate in a double boiler over hot water and spread over fudge layer. Cut shortbread into squares just before chocolate hardens.

MAKES ABOUT 50

Clockwise from bottom left: *Rich Chocolate Chip Cookies, Cheesy Barbecue Biscuits, Spicy Biscuits, Millionaire's Shortbread.*

19
BISCUITS AND RUSKS

RUSKS

Rusks can be made with white flour, wholemeal flour, or a mixture of the two. Butter gives a better flavour, but if you want to store the rusks for longer, use margarine.

Dry out rusks overnight in the oven at its lowest setting (about 50 °C/ 120 °F). Use a spoon to keep the oven door ajar so moisture can escape. Allow rusks to cool completely before storing (for up to three months) in an airtight container.

MUESLI RUSKS

700 g (1½ lb) butter or margarine
750 ml (1¼ pints) buttermilk
400 g (14 oz) caster sugar
4 large eggs, beaten
1.35 kg (3 lb) self-raising flour
3 tbsp baking powder
1½ tsp salt
300 g (10½ oz) All-Bran flakes
300 g (10½ oz) muesli

1 Melt butter in a heavy-based saucepan. Add buttermilk and sugar. Remove from heat and add eggs.

2 Sift flour, baking powder and salt into a large bowl. Add All-Bran flakes, muesli and butter mixture. Mix well.

3 Shape into balls and pack into two large, greased roasting tins. Bake in a preheated oven at 180 °C (350 °F, gas mark 4) for 45 minutes. Turn onto a rack to cool slightly; break up while still warm. Dry out overnight in the oven on its lowest setting.

MAKES ABOUT 140, DEPENDING ON SIZE

LIGHT BRAN RUSKS

875 g (1 lb 15 oz) self-raising flour
1 tsp salt
30 g (1 oz) wheat bran
250 g (8½ oz) butter or margarine
2 large eggs
125 g (4½ oz) caster sugar
500 ml (17 fl oz) buttermilk

1 Sift flour and salt. Add bran. Rub in butter until mixture resembles breadcrumbs. Beat eggs, sugar and buttermilk together. Add liquid mixture to dry mixture. Mix well.

2 Shape into balls and pack into a large, greased roasting tin.

3 Bake in a preheated oven at 180 °C (350 °F, gas mark 4) for about 50 minutes. Turn out onto a wire rack to cool slightly. Break up while still warm, and leave to cool further. Dry out overnight in the oven on its lowest setting.

MAKES ABOUT 50, DEPENDING ON SIZE

BUTTERMILK-COCONUT RUSKS

1.35 kg (3 lb) self-raising flour
1 tsp salt
600 g (1 lb 5 oz) caster sugar
120 g (4¼ oz) desiccated coconut
2 tbsp aniseed (optional)
375 g (13 oz) butter or margarine
3 large eggs
500 ml (17 fl oz) buttermilk

1 Sift flour. Add salt, sugar, coconut and aniseed and rub in butter. Add eggs and buttermilk. Mix well and roll into balls. Pack into greased roasting tins.

2 Bake in a preheated oven at 180 °C (350 °F, gas mark 4) for 45 minutes until golden brown.

3 Turn onto a rack to cool slightly; break up while still warm. Dry out overnight in the oven on its lowest setting.

MAKES ABOUT 80, DEPENDING ON SIZE

BUTTERMILK RUSKS

1.8 kg (4 lb) self-raising flour
2 tsp salt
1 tbsp baking powder
750 g (1 lb 10 oz) butter or margarine
400 g (14 oz) caster sugar
2 tbsp aniseed (optional)
1 litre (1¾ pints) buttermilk
3 large eggs

1 Sift flour, salt and baking powder. Rub in butter until mixture resembles breadcrumbs. Add sugar and aniseed.

2 Mix buttermilk and eggs together. Add to dry ingredients and mix well.

3 Shape into balls and pack into large, greased roasting tins. Bake in a preheated oven at 180 °C (350 °F, gas mark 4) for 50–60 minutes.

4 Turn onto a rack to cool slightly; break up while still warm. Dry out overnight in the oven on its lowest setting.

MAKES ABOUT 140, DEPENDING ON SIZE

Left to right: *Light Bran Rusks, Butternut Rusks, Muesli Rusks.*

BUTTERNUT RUSKS

750 ml (1¼ pints) boiling water
300 g (10½ oz) caster sugar
325 g (11 oz) butter or margarine
3 large eggs, beaten
875 g (1 lb 15 oz) wholemeal
or brown flour
8 tsp baking powder
2 tsp salt
1 tsp cream of tartar
375 g (13 oz) cooked, mashed
butternut squash

1 Combine boiling water, sugar and butter and stir until sugar has melted. Leave mixture to cool then add eggs.

2 Sift flour, baking powder, salt and cream of tartar together and add to egg mixture. Add bran from sieve and mix well. (The mixture will be runny.)

3 Add mashed squash and mix well.

4 Pour into three greased 23 cm (9 in) loaf tins. Bake in a preheated oven at 180 °C (350 °F, gas mark 4) for about 1 hour.

5 Leave in tins for a few minutes to cool, then turn out onto a wire rack to cool completely. Cut each loaf into thick slices and divide each slice into three again.

6 Dry out overnight in the oven at its lowest setting.

MAKES ABOUT 70, DEPENDING ON SIZE

TIPS

- Use an electric knife to slice the rusks to prevent breakage.
- Instead of drying them out in the oven, leave the rusks to stand on a wire rack overnight and cut the next day. They won't break up and crumble as much.

BARS, SQUARES AND SWEET TREATS

These recipes, a cross between a biscuit and a cake, are ideal when you want to indulge in something small and snacky.
They are mostly baked in trays and then cut into slices or squares. Storing and freezing rules are the same as for cakes.

CHERRY DREAM BARS

80 g (2¾ oz) soft butter or margarine
50 g (1¾ oz) light brown sugar
125 g (4½ oz) plain flour

TOPPING
2 large eggs
200 g (7 oz) light brown sugar
30 g (1 oz) plain flour
½ tsp baking powder
120 g (4¼ oz) desiccated coconut
75 g (2½ oz) red glacé cherries,
halved
1 tsp vanilla essence

1 Cream butter and sugar. Sift flour
and add. Press mixture into a greased
20 cm (8 in) square baking tin. Bake in
a preheated oven at 180 °C (350 °F,
gas mark 4) for 12 minutes. Set aside.

2 For topping: beat eggs and sugar
together. Sift flour and baking powder
and add to egg mixture with all the
remaining ingredients. Mix thoroughly.

3 Spread this mixture over the warm
cake and bake for 15–20 minutes until
light brown. Cut into squares. Cool
in the tin for a few minutes before
transferring to a rack to cool further.

MAKES ABOUT 18

VARIATION
Substitute cherries with 75 g
(2½ oz) chopped walnuts.

CHOCOLATE-NUT SQUARES

125 g (4½ oz) butter
150 g (5½ oz) light brown sugar
1 large egg
1 tsp vanilla essence
125 g (4½ oz) plain flour
1 tsp baking powder
scant ½ tsp salt
40 g (1¼ oz) desiccated coconut
50 g (1¾ oz) coarsely chopped
pecan nuts or walnuts
60 g (2 oz) chocolate chips

TOPPING
2 tbsp chopped pecan nuts

1 Cream butter and sugar. Add egg
and vanilla essence and beat until
light and fluffy.

2 Sift the flour, baking powder and
salt. Add it to the mixture along with
the coconut, nuts and chocolate chips.
Mix well.

3 Spoon mixture into a greased
16 x 26 cm (6½ x 10½ in) tray bake
tin. Sprinkle extra nuts on top.

4 Bake in a preheated oven at
180 °C (350 °F, gas mark 4) for about
25 minutes and cut into squares.

MAKES ABOUT 24

BUTTERHORNS

250 g (8½ oz) soft butter or
margarine
375 g (13 oz) sieved cottage
cheese
250 g (8½ oz) plain flour
scant ½ tsp salt

ICING
130 g (4¾ oz) icing sugar
2 tbsp milk

1 Cream butter and cottage cheese.
Sift flour and salt and mix into the
butter mixture. Refrigerate for at least
4 hours, or overnight. Divide into four
pieces and roll each piece out to a
thickness of 3 mm (⅛ in).

2 Cut into wedges (about 14 cm/
5½ in long) and roll each wedge,
starting at the wide end (about
11 cm/4½ in wide) to pointed end.
Place on greased baking trays. Bake
in a preheated oven at 190 °C (375 °F,
gas mark 5) for 12–15 minutes.

3 For icing: mix icing sugar and milk.
Drizzle icing over butterhorns while
still warm.

MAKES ABOUT 22

TIP
When creaming butter for baking,
rinse the bowl with boiling water
to make the task a lot easier.

Cherry Dream Bars

GRANOLA BARS

160 g (5¾ oz) butter or margarine
100 g (3½ oz) honey or
golden syrup
200 g (7 oz) caster sugar
160 g (5¾ oz) rolled oats
100 g (3½ oz) plain flour
1 tsp ground cinnamon
50 g (1¾ oz) pecan nuts or walnuts
50 g (1¾ oz) seedless raisins
75 g (2½ oz) dried mango, chopped
75 g (2½ oz) dried apricots, chopped
50 g (1¾ oz) ground almonds
(optional)
2 tbsp sesame seeds

1 Melt butter and honey in a pan over low heat, then stir in the sugar.

2 Keep the heat low until sugar has dissolved, then bring to the boil for 1–2 minutes, stirring, until thickened and smooth.

3 Mix together all the remaining ingredients and stir into the syrup until well combined. Press into a greased 16 x 26 cm (6½ x 10½ in) tray bake tin. Press down lightly.

4 Bake in a preheated oven at 180 °C (350 °F, gas mark 4) for 25–30 minutes until just beginning to brown. Leave to cool and cut into bars or squares.

MAKES ABOUT 18

TIP
When honey or golden syrup has crystallised, remove the lid and place the jar in the microwave on high for about 30 seconds, then stir until it becomes smooth.

DECADENT BROWNIES

120 g (4¼ oz) dark chocolate
200 g (7 oz) butter or
margarine
3 large eggs
210 g (7½ oz) caster sugar
1 tsp vanilla essence
60 g (2 oz) self-raising flour
2 tbsp cocoa powder
scant ½ tsp salt
75 g (2½ oz) chopped walnuts
(optional)

1 Melt chocolate and butter in a pan, then set aside to cool slightly.

2 Beat eggs and sugar until light and fluffy. Add vanilla essence and gradually beat in the melted mixture.

3 Sift the flour, cocoa powder and salt over the mixture, then fold it in together with the walnuts (if using).

4 Turn the mixture into a greased 16 x 26 cm (6½ x 10½ in) tray bake tin. Bake in a preheated oven at 190 °C (375 °F, gas mark 5) for 20–25 minutes or until just firm in the centre.

5 Leave to cool in the tin for a few minutes, then cut into squares and turn out onto a wire rack to cool.

MAKES ABOUT 28

TIP
When baking brownies, be careful not to over-bake them. When you insert a skewer into the centre, a tiny amount of moist mixture should adhere to it, otherwise the texture will be too dry.

GINGER SQUARES

80 g (2¾ oz) butter or margarine
85 g (3 oz) honey
65 g (2¼ oz) light brown sugar
100 ml (3½ fl oz) milk
2 large eggs
185 g (6½ oz) self-raising flour
1 tbsp ground ginger
scant ½ tsp bicarbonate of soda

ICING
60 g (2 oz) butter or margarine
100 g (3½ oz) light brown sugar
2 tbsp milk
100 g (3½ oz) icing sugar

1 Place butter, honey and sugar in a saucepan. Stir over low heat (do not boil) until sugar dissolves. Cool slightly.

2 Stir milk, eggs, flour, ginger and bicarbonate of soda into mixture. Pour into a greased 16 x 26 cm (6½ x 10½ in) tray bake tin and bake in a preheated oven at 180 °C (350 °F, gas mark 4) for 25–30 minutes. Leave to stand for 5 minutes before turning onto a wire rack to cool.

3 For icing: melt butter in a small saucepan. Add brown sugar and milk, bring to the boil, then simmer, stirring, for 2 minutes. Stir in enough icing sugar to make a spreadable consistency. Spread over cake and cut into squares.

MAKES 24

Clockwise from left: *Decadent Brownies, Ginger Squares, Granola Bars.*

GRANADILLA ÉCLAIRS

60 g (2 oz) butter
125 ml (4 fl oz) water
60 g (2 oz) plain flour
2 large eggs, lightly beaten

FILLING
250 ml (8½ fl oz) double cream
35 g (1¼ oz) icing sugar
115 g (4 oz) granadilla or passion
fruit pulp

1 Place butter and water in a saucepan and heat until melted. Bring to the boil and remove from heat. Sift flour and add. Stir well with a wooden spoon until the mixture forms a ball in the centre of the saucepan. Leave to cool slightly. Add eggs, one at a time, beating well after each addition, until the pastry is smooth.

2 Pipe onto a greased baking tray and bake in a preheated oven at 200 °C (400 °F, gas mark 6) for 18–20 minutes until puffed and golden. Remove and cut a slit in the side to let steam escape. Return to oven for 2 minutes to dry out. Transfer to a wire rack to cool.

3 For filling: whip cream until stiff and add sugar and fruit pulp. Spoon or pipe the filling into the éclairs. Dust with extra icing sugar.

MAKES ABOUT 12

VARIATION
Fill with whipped cream and top with chocolate icing – 50 g (1¾ oz) chocolate, melted, 15 g (½ oz) butter, 240 g (8¼ oz) icing sugar.

STICKY CARAMEL APPLE PIECES

3 medium Granny Smith apples

BATTER
100 g (3½ oz) plain flour
scant ½ tsp salt
1 tbsp sunflower oil
100 ml (3½ fl oz) warm water
2 large egg whites
oil for deep-frying

SAUCE
125 g (4½ oz) butter
200 g (7 oz) soft brown sugar
125 ml (4 fl oz) double cream

1 Peel and core apples and cut each one into 8–12 pieces.

2 For batter: sift flour and salt. Add oil and water. Whisk the egg whites until soft peaks form and fold in to make a smooth batter. Mix well and leave to stand for 30 minutes.

3 Coat the apple pieces in batter and deep-fry in hot oil until golden brown. Drain on paper towel.

4 For sauce: heat butter and sugar until the sugar has dissolved. Add the cream and bring to the boil, stirring for a few minutes. Pour the sauce over apple pieces and serve immediately.

MAKES 24–36 PIECES

VARIATION
Substitute the apples with four sliced bananas.

TRUFFLES

200 g (7 oz) vanilla or chocolate
cake crumbs
50 g (1¾ oz) pecan nuts, chopped
40 g (1¼ oz) desiccated coconut
52 g (2 oz) caster sugar
scant ½ tsp rum essence
30 g (1 oz) butter
150 g (5½ oz) dark chocolate
caster sugar, cocoa powder
or melted chocolate for rolling

1 Mix all ingredients together except butter and chocolate.

2 Melt butter and chocolate and mix thoroughly with other ingredients. Roll teaspoonfuls of mixture into balls and roll in sugar, cocoa or melted chocolate.

MAKES ABOUT 30

TIPS
- To make the truffles, use crumbs from trimmed off-cuts, flopped cakes or even stale pieces of cake.
- The secret to melting chocolate is to melt it slowly over low heat in a double boiler. Alternatively, heat at 50% power in a 750 watt microwave for 2–4 minutes. (The time required will depend on volume.) Stir after each minute until shiny and melted.

Clockwise from left: *Granadilla Éclairs, Sticky Caramel Apple Pieces, Truffles.*

BRANDY SNAP ROLLS

160 g (5¾ oz) caster sugar
125 g (4½ oz) butter
65 g (2¼ oz) golden syrup
125 g (4½ oz) plain flour
1 tsp ground ginger
1 tsp fresh lemon juice
2 tbsp brandy

FILLING
125 ml (4 fl oz) double cream
1 tbsp caster sugar

1 Heat the sugar, butter and syrup together until the sugar dissolves. Remove from heat. Sift the flour and ginger and stir it into butter mixture. Add lemon juice and brandy and stir until smooth.

2 Place heaped teaspoonfuls well apart on greased baking trays.

3 Bake in a preheated oven at 160 °C (325 °F, gas mark 3) for 8–10 minutes until golden brown. Remove from oven and leave for a few seconds to cool.

4 As soon as you're able to handle the snaps, roll them around the handles of greased wooden spoons.

5 For filling: whip cream and sugar until stiff and pipe into or fill rolls.

MAKES ABOUT 20

VARIATION
Create baskets by pressing the snaps over oranges or something round. Fill with fresh fruit, berries and cream or custard.

CHEWY APRICOT BARS

125 g (4½ oz) self-raising flour
1 tsp ground cinnamon
scant ½ tsp salt
4 tbsp wheat bran
65 g (2¼ oz) light brown sugar
100 g (3½ oz) dried apricots, chopped
50 g (1¾ oz) chopped walnuts or pecan nuts
85 g (3 oz) golden syrup or honey
2 tbsp milk

1 Sift flour, cinnamon and salt together. Add bran.

2 Add sugar, apricots and nuts. Add syrup and milk and mix well.

3 Spread the mixture in a greased 20 cm (8 in) square cake tin and bake in a preheated oven at 180 °C (350 °F, gas mark 4) for 20–25 minutes. Remove from oven and cut into bars or squares.

MAKES ABOUT 15

CHOCOLATE-COCONUT SLICES

250 g (8½ oz) butter or margarine
100 g (3½ oz) caster sugar
250 g (8½ oz) plain flour
3 tbsp cocoa powder
160 g (5¾ oz) desiccated coconut

TOPPING
100 g (3½ oz) butter or margarine
250 g (8½ oz) icing sugar
32 g (1 oz) cocoa powder
1 tbsp milk

1 Cream butter and sugar. Sift the flour and cocoa, add coconut and mix it all into the butter mixture.

2 Press into a greased 23 x 32 cm (9 x 13 in) Swiss roll tin.

3 Bake in a preheated oven at 180 °C (350 °F, gas mark 4) for 20–25 minutes.

4 For topping: melt butter in a heavy-based saucepan and add icing sugar and cocoa. Add milk and mix well. Remove from heat and spread over base while still warm. Cut into slices.

MAKES ABOUT 40

CHERRY BALLS

100 g (3½ oz) self-raising flour
50 g (1¾ oz) butter or margarine
52 g (2 oz) caster sugar
1 large egg, beaten
1 tbsp milk
about 15 glacé cherries
oil for deep-frying
210 g (7½ oz) caster sugar for rolling

1 Sift the flour and rub in butter. Add sugar.

2 Add beaten egg and milk to flour and mix to a soft dough.

3 Form balls of dough with cherries inside. Deep-fry in hot oil until golden brown and drain on kitchen paper. Roll in caster sugar.

MAKES ABOUT 15

Clockwise from top left: *Chocolate-Coconut Slices, Chewy Apricot Bars, Cherry Balls.*

KOEKSISTERS

SYRUP

1 kg (2¼ lb) granulated sugar
500 ml (17 fl oz) water
2 pieces root ginger, slightly bruised
pinch of cream of tartar
pinch of salt
1 tsp grated lemon rind
125 ml (4 fl oz) fresh lemon juice

DOUGH

250 g (8½ oz) plain flour
4 tsp baking powder
½ tsp salt
30 g (1 oz) butter
125 ml (4 fl oz) buttermilk or water
with lemon juice
oil for deep-frying

1 For syrup: place all ingredients in a saucepan and stir over low heat until the sugar has dissolved. Cover and boil for a few minutes. Do not stir. Remove from heat and chill.

2 For dough: sift the dry ingredients together and rub in the butter until mixture resembles breadcrumbs.

3 Add the liquid and mix to a soft dough. Knead until smooth.

4 Cover and leave to stand for about 15 minutes. Roll to a thickness of 5 mm (¼ in) and cut into strips of 5 cm (2 in) in width and 7 cm (scant 3 in) in length. Starting 1 cm (½ in) from the top, cut each strip into three.

5 Plait together three strips at a time and press the ends firmly together.

6 Deep-fry in hot oil until golden and well-done. Drain on kitchen paper and dip into ice-cold syrup.

MAKES ABOUT 24

TIPS
- To check if oil is hot enough for frying, dip a cube of bread into the oil – it should turn brown within 90 seconds.
- Koeksisters freeze successfully in an airtight container. Remove from the freezer 30 minutes before serving.

QUICK LOAVES AND LARGE CAKES

The aroma from the oven and the taste of freshly baked cakes still make all of us appreciate Mum! Round cake tins are still the most widely used for cakes, but square tins, loaf tins and large rectangular tins are popular too. The cake mixture should only reach to half to two-thirds of the tin, leaving enough space for the cake to rise. For successful cakes, use only the best ingredients at room temperature, and weigh and measure accurately. Also take care with the lining and greasing of the tins.

WHISKING

Place eggs and sugar in a large bowl and whisk until light and thick. If not using an electric mixer, set the bowl over a pan of hot water. Sponges made using this method are very light in texture.

CREAMING

Preferably use an electric mixer, as vigorous beating will be required when mixing by hand or with a wooden spoon. Beat soft butter and sugar together until light and creamy – it should have a very smooth consistency. Beat the eggs into the creamed mixture, one at a time, beating well after each addition. To prevent curdling, add a little flour to the eggs.

FOLDING IN

Sift the flour over the creamed or whisked cake mixture, holding the sieve above the mixture to let it fall and aerate. Use a large metal spoon or whisk, cutting and carefully folding the flour into the mixture using a figure of eight movement.

LINING TINS

For sponges, place tin on greaseproof paper, draw around it and cut out 5 cm (2 in) wider around the base. Snip the lining at intervals. Lining for sides should be placed first, then the base. Grease the tin as well as the paper. Special baking parchment can also be used. Even non-stick tins need greasing, and this can be done by brushing on butter or spraying the tin with non-stick spray. Flour can also be dusted on to prevent sticking.

TESTING GUIDELINES

– When a sponge pulls away from the sides of the tin, it is done.
– A quick loaf is baked when the top looks and feels firm and dry.
– A cake is ready when a cake tester inserted into the centre comes out dry. If the centre is still raw, return to the oven for a further 5–8 minutes.
– Loaves with a soft, cake-like texture can be left to stand for 10 minutes to firm up slightly before being turned out onto a wire rack to cool.

STORING

Cakes should be cooled to room temperature before storing in an airtight container. Quick loaves and un-iced cakes keep well for up to three months if frozen in airtight freezer film or bags. Leave the loaves to thaw at room temperature before serving. If icing is not used, dust icing sugar over the top for an appealing finish before serving. Freeze whisked sponges for up to one month only.
Cakes such as Madeira keep well for up to four days if sealed tightly. Fruit cakes and gingerbread actually improve with age. Most cakes, however, are enjoyed freshly baked.

ICING

Icing adds colour and flavour to cakes and prevents them from drying out. Only ice cakes once completely cool.
Some icings are spread over the cake, others are poured over. Do not over-mix the icing as it will become runny. Use a palette knife dipped in hot water for easy spreading. For a textured effect, draw a palette knife forwards and backwards across the cake. Once a cake has been iced, the sides can be coated with grated chocolate or chopped or flaked nuts.

BASIC BUTTER ICING

100 g (3½ oz) soft butter
250 g (8½ oz) icing sugar
2 tsp vanilla essence
about 5 tsp milk

1 Cream butter, icing sugar and vanilla essence. Add enough milk to make mixture light and creamy, and of a spreadable consistency.

2 Sandwich the layers of cake together with icing, then ice the top.

VARIATION

Omit vanilla essence and add grated citrus rind, fresh citrus juice, sieved cottage cheese, cocoa powder or coffee powder.

Meringue Cake (page 44)

PINEAPPLE CAKE

CAKE
125 g (4½ oz) butter or margarine
210 g (7½ oz) caster sugar
2 large eggs
375 g (13 oz) self-raising flour
80 ml (2¾ fl oz) milk

FILLING
440 g can crushed pineapple
210 g (7½ oz) caster sugar
2 large eggs, lightly beaten
30 g (1 oz) custard powder

1 For cake: cream the butter and sugar. Add eggs and beat until light and fluffy.

2 Sift flour and add, alternately with milk, to egg mixture. Divide between four lined and greased 23 cm (9 in) cake tins. Level with a palette knife.

3 Bake in a preheated oven at 180 °C (350 °F, gas mark 4) for about 20 minutes until light brown. Leave to cool slightly in the tin, then turn out onto a wire rack to cool.

4 For filling: boil pineapple, sugar and eggs for 3 minutes, stirring constantly.

5 Mix custard powder with a little cold water and stir into pineapple mixture. Boil until thick. Leave to cool.

6 Spread filling over three of the cakes and stack them on top of each other. Crumble the remaining cake and spread over the top. Store in an airtight container for 24 hours before serving.

MAKES 1 LARGE CAKE

MADEIRA COCONUT LOAF

125 g (4½ oz) butter
80 g (2¾ oz) caster sugar
3 large egg yolks
1 tsp vanilla essence
125 g (4½ oz) plain flour
2 tsp baking powder
pinch of salt
100 ml (3½ fl oz) milk

TOPPING
3 large egg whites
80 g (2¾ oz) caster sugar
80 g (2¾ oz) desiccated coconut

1 Cream butter and sugar. Add egg yolks, one at a time, beating well after each addition, until light and fluffy. Add vanilla essence.

2 Sift flour, baking powder and salt and add, alternately with milk, to butter mixture.

3 Spoon the mixture into a greased 23 cm (9 in) loaf tin.

4 For topping: whisk egg whites until stiff. Add sugar and beat well. Add coconut and mix. Spoon on top of cake mixture.

5 Bake in a preheated oven at 180 °C (350 °F, gas mark 4) for 30 minutes. Reduce temperature to 160 °C (325 °F, gas mark 3) and bake for another 15–20 minutes. Turn out onto a wire rack to cool.

MAKES 1 LOAF

BANANA LOAF

125 g (4½ oz) butter or margarine
200 g (7 oz) caster sugar
2 large eggs
1 tsp vanilla essence
250 g (8½ oz) plain flour
1 tsp baking powder
pinch of salt
1 tsp bicarbonate of soda
3–4 mashed ripe bananas
2 tbsp fresh lemon juice

1 Cream butter and sugar. Add eggs, one at a time, beating well after each addition. Add vanilla essence.

2 Sift dry ingredients and mix into butter mixture along with mashed banana and lemon juice.

3 Spoon into a greased 23 cm (9 in) loaf tin. Bake in a preheated oven at 180 °C (350 °F, gas mark 4) for 1 hour. Turn out onto a wire rack to cool.

MAKES 1 LOAF

VARIATIONS
Substitute half plain white flour with wholemeal flour and add 50 g (1¾ oz) chopped pecan nuts or walnuts.
Substitute vanilla essence with almond essence.

Clockwise from top left: *Madeira Coconut Loaf, Banana Loaf, Pineapple Cake.*

QUICK LOAVES AND LARGE CAKES

APRICOT SWISS ROLL

4 large eggs
3 tbsp apricot juice
210 g (7½ oz) caster sugar
125 g (4½ oz) plain flour
2 tsp baking powder
pinch of salt
caster sugar for rolling
about 110 g (scant 4 oz) smooth
apricot jam

1 Beat eggs until light and fluffy,
then beat in apricot juice. Add sugar
gradually and beat until dissolved.

2 Sift the dry ingredients in thin
layers over the egg mixture and fold
in lightly with a spatula. Repeat until
all the dry ingredients have been used.
Spoon the mixture into a greased
and lined 23 x 32 cm (9 x 13 in)
Swiss roll tin.

3 Bake in a preheated oven at 200 °C
(400 °F, gas mark 6) for 10–12 minutes.
Turn onto a clean, dry tea towel
sprinkled with caster sugar. Trim edges
to ensure rolling without breaking.

4 Spread a thin layer of apricot jam
over the cake. Roll up and wrap in the
towel. Leave for a minute or two, then
remove towel and leave to cool.

MAKES 1 CAKE

VARIATION
Chocolate roll: Substitute 4 tbsp
flour with 3 tbsp cocoa powder.
Use strong, black coffee instead
of juice. Roll cake with buttered
waxed paper, cool, unroll and fill
with whipped cream. Roll up.

ORANGE AND COURGETTE LOAF

100 g (3½ oz) caster sugar
100 ml (3½ fl oz) sunflower oil or
melted butter
1 large egg
1 tsp vanilla essence
250 g (8½ oz) self-raising flour
scant ½ tsp bicarbonate of soda
1 tsp ground cinnamon
scant ½ tsp salt
pinch of grated nutmeg
pinch of ground cloves
4 tbsp wheat bran
1 tbsp grated orange rind
125 ml (4 fl oz) fresh orange juice
135 g (scant 5 oz) grated
courgettes
50 g (1¾ oz) chopped walnuts
75 g (2½ oz) seedless raisins

1 Beat sugar, oil and egg until
light and fluffy. Add vanilla essence.
Sift all dry ingredients and add to
mixture, with bran.

2 Add remaining ingredients and
mix well. Spoon into a greased 23 cm
(9 in) loaf tin.

3 Bake in a preheated oven at
180 °C (350 °F, gas mark 4) for
35–45 minutes. Turn out onto a
wire rack to cool.

MAKES 1 LOAF

TIP
To make vanilla sugar, pour some
caster sugar into a clean jar and
add a vanilla pod. Store in a cool,
dark place for about a week to
allow the flavour to develop.

SOURED CREAM CINNAMON CAKE

250 ml (8½ fl oz) soured cream
1 tsp bicarbonate of soda
125 g (4½ oz) butter or margarine
100 g (3½ oz) caster sugar
2 large eggs
1 tsp vanilla essence
250 g (8½ oz) plain flour
2 tsp baking powder

TOPPING
50 g (1¾ oz) brown sugar
1 tsp ground cinnamon
25 g (scant 1 oz) pecan nuts,
chopped

1 Mix soured cream and bicarbonate
of soda in a bowl. Set aside.

2 Cream butter and sugar. Add eggs
and vanilla essence and beat well until
light and fluffy.

3 Sift dry ingredients. Add to butter
mixture, with the soured cream. Spoon
half the mixture into a greased 23 cm
(9 in) loose-bottomed round cake tin.

4 For topping: mix all ingredients
together. Sprinkle half the topping
mixture over the cake. Cover with
remaining mixture, then sprinkle over
remainder of the topping. Bake in a
preheated oven at 180 °C (350 °F,
gas mark 4) for 35–45 minutes.
Serve warm or cold.

MAKES 1 CAKE

TIP
This delicious cake will stay moist
for up to two days.

Left to right: *Soured Cream Cinnamon Cake, Orange and Courgette Loaf.*

POPPYSEED DELIGHT

3 large eggs
200 g (7 oz) caster sugar
125 ml (4 fl oz) sunflower oil or
melted butter
125 g (4½ oz) self-raising flour
175 ml (6 fl oz) plain yoghurt
40 g (1¼ oz) desiccated coconut
4 tbsp poppyseeds

LEMON ICING
30 g (1 oz) soft butter
200 g (7 oz) icing sugar
1 tsp grated lemon rind
2–3 tbsp fresh lemon juice

1 Beat the eggs and sugar until
light and fluffy.

2 Add oil and beat well. Sift flour
and add, along with the yoghurt,
coconut and poppyseeds.

3 Pour into a greased 24 cm (9½ in)
square cake tin or ovenproof dish.
Bake in a preheated oven at 180 °C
(350 °F, gas mark 4) for 35–40 minutes.
Leave to cool in the container.

4 For icing: cream butter, icing sugar
and rind. Add enough juice to mixture
to make it light and creamy, and of a
spreadable consistency. Ice the top of
the cake and cut into squares.

MAKES ABOUT 16 SQUARES

TIP
When only a few drops of orange
or lemon juice are required, use a
thick skewer to pierce the skin in a
few places and squeeze the fruit
for juice to run out.

BUTTERMILK CAKE

125 g (4½ oz) butter
200 g (7 oz) light brown sugar
2 large eggs
1 tsp vanilla essence
250 g (8½ oz) self-raising flour
scant ½ tsp salt
250 ml (8½ fl oz) buttermilk
75 g (2½ oz) currants
icing sugar for dusting

1 Cream butter and sugar. Add eggs
and vanilla essence and beat well until
light and fluffy.

2 Sift flour and salt and add,
alternately with buttermilk, to sugar
mixture. Add currants, mixing well.

3 Spoon into a greased 23 cm (9 in)
loaf tin. Bake in a preheated oven
at 160 °C (325 °F, gas mark 3) for
50–60 minutes.

4 Turn out onto a wire rack to cool.
Dust with icing sugar.

MAKES 1 LOAF

PRUNE CAKE

125 g (4½ oz) butter or margarine
200 g (7 oz) caster sugar
3 large eggs
150 g (5½ oz) pitted prunes
250 g (8½ oz) plain flour
1 tbsp baking powder
scant ½ tsp bicarbonate of soda
1 tsp ground allspice
1 tsp ground cinnamon
scant ½ tsp salt
125 ml (4 fl oz) buttermilk
200 ml (7 fl oz) apple juice

CREAM CHEESE ICING
100 g (3½ oz) butter
400 g (14 oz) icing sugar
125 g (4½ oz) sieved cottage cheese
1 tsp vanilla essence
chopped nuts to decorate

1 Cream butter and sugar. Add eggs,
one at a time, beating well after each
addition until light and fluffy. Chop
the prunes as fine as possible and add.

2 Sift dry ingredients together and
add, alternately with buttermilk and
apple juice, to egg mixture.

3 Pour into two greased 20 cm (8 in)
round cake tins. Bake in a preheated
oven at 180 °C (350 °F, gas mark 4) for
30–35 minutes. Cool on a rack.

4 For icing: cream butter, then add
icing sugar and remaining ingredients.
Mix until blended; do not overmix as it
will become runny. Ice the cooled cake
and decorate with chopped nuts.

MAKES 1 LARGE CAKE

VARIATION
Substitute cottage cheese with
mashed banana for an alternative
delicious icing.

Left to right: *Sweet Potato Loaf, Poppyseed Delight, Prune Cake.*

SWEET POTATO LOAF

200 g (7 oz) butter or margarine
100 g (3½ oz) brown sugar
2 large eggs
65 g (2¼ oz) golden syrup or
honey
250 g (8½ oz) self-raising flour
1½ tsp ground ginger
1 tsp ground cinnamon
200 g (7 oz) cooked, mashed
sweet potato

CARAMEL ICING
60 g (2 oz) soft butter
40 g (1¼ oz) brown sugar
200 g (7 oz) icing sugar
1 tsp caramel essence
about 5 tsp milk

1 Cream butter and sugar. Add eggs, one at a time, beating until light and fluffy. Beat in golden syrup.

2 Sift dry ingredients and add, with cold sweet potato, to mixture. Spoon into a greased 23 cm (9 in) loaf tin.

3 Bake in a preheated oven at 180 °C (350 °F, gas mark 4) for 40–45 minutes. Leave for a few minutes in tin before turning onto a wire rack to cool.

4 For icing: cream butter and sugar. Add icing sugar, caramel essence and enough milk to make icing light and creamy. Ice the top of the loaf.

MAKES 1 LOAF

VARIATION
Instead of icing the cake, dust icing sugar over the top.

TIP
If icing is too soft, cornflour or custard powder can be added to stiffen it up if no more icing sugar is available.

BEETROOT AND CARROT CAKE

200 g (7 oz) caster sugar
250 ml (8½ fl oz) corn or
sunflower oil
3 large eggs, separated
2 tsp caramel essence
250 g (8½ oz) plain flour
pinch of salt
2 tsp baking powder
125 g (4½ oz) grated raw beetroot
125 g (4½ oz) grated raw carrots
4 tbsp milk

SYRUP
100 g (3½ oz) granulated sugar
125 ml (4 fl oz) water
scant ½ tsp caramel essence

1 Beat sugar, oil and egg yolks.
Add caramel essence.

2 Sift dry ingredients and beat
into sugar mixture. Whisk egg whites
until soft peaks form and fold into
sugar mixture.

3 Add grated beetroot, carrots and
milk and mix well. Spoon mixture
into a greased 23 cm (9 in) loose-
bottomed springform tin.

4 Bake in a preheated oven at 180 °C
(350 °F, gas mark 4) for 25–30 minutes.

5 For syrup: boil sugar and water
until sugar dissolves. Remove from
heat, add caramel essence and pour
syrup over the cake as soon as it
comes out of the oven.

MAKES 1 LARGE CAKE

LEMON LOAF

125 g (4½ oz) butter or margarine
200 g (7 oz) caster sugar
2 large eggs
1 tsp grated lemon rind
170 g (6 oz) plain flour
2 tsp baking powder
scant ½ tsp salt
125 ml (4 fl oz) milk

TOPPING
50 g (1¾ oz) granulated sugar
125 ml (4 fl oz) fresh lemon juice

1 Cream butter and sugar. Beat in
eggs and rind. Sift the dry ingredients
together and add, alternately with
milk, to creamed mixture. Spoon into
a greased 23 cm (9 in) loaf tin.

2 Bake in a preheated oven at 180 °C
(350 °F, gas mark 4) for 40–45 minutes,
or until done. Cool in tin.

3 For topping: boil sugar and lemon
juice for about 3 minutes. Spoon
syrup over loaf in tin while still hot.
Leave cake for a few more minutes
in tin before turning out onto a wire
rack to cool further.

MAKES 1 LOAF

> **TIP**
> A medium lemon yields about
> 1 tbsp grated rind and 3 tbsp juice.

HONEY CAKE

30 g (1 oz) butter or margarine
80 g (2¾ oz) caster sugar
1 large egg
125 g (4½ oz) plain flour
1 tbsp baking powder
125 ml (4 fl oz) milk

TOPPING
80 g (2¾ oz) butter
85 g (3 oz) honey

1 Cream butter and sugar. Add egg
and beat until light and fluffy.

2 Sift dry ingredients and add,
with milk, to butter mixture. Mix well.
Spoon mixture into a greased 23 cm
(9 in) round or rectangular ovenproof
dish. Bake in a preheated oven at
180 °C (350 °F, gas mark 4) for
20–25 minutes.

3 For topping: melt butter and honey
in a saucepan and pour syrup over
cake while still hot. Cut the cake into
wedges or squares and serve.

MAKES 1 CAKE

> **TIP**
> To measure honey, set saucepan on
> scale, set to zero, then add honey.

Left to right: *Lemon Loaf, Beetroot and Carrot Cake.*

PEANUT BUTTER LOAF

180 g (6¼ oz) crunchy or
smooth peanut butter
100 g (3½ oz) soft butter
250 g (8½ oz) plain flour
100 g (3½ oz) caster sugar
2 tsp baking powder
scant ½ tsp salt
200 ml (7 fl oz) milk
2 tsp grated orange rind
2 large eggs, beaten

1 Mix peanut butter and butter. Sift
dry ingredients and mix into peanut
butter mixture. Add milk, rind and
eggs and mix well.

2 Spoon into a greased 23 cm (9 in)
loaf tin. Bake in a preheated oven at
180 °C (350 °F, gas mark 4) for about
50 minutes. Cool in tin for 10 minutes
and transfer to a rack to cool further.

MAKES 1 LOAF

BUTTER CAKE

125 g (4½ oz) butter
210 g (7½ oz) caster sugar
4 large eggs, separated
1 tsp vanilla essence
250 g (8½ oz) plain flour
2 tsp baking powder
pinch of salt
125 ml (4 fl oz) milk
80 ml (2¾ fl oz) water
1 tsp cream of tartar

BUTTER ICING
125 g (4½ oz) butter
200 g (7 oz) icing sugar
1 tsp vanilla essence
1 tbsp milk, if required

1 Cream the butter and sugar. Add
the egg yolks and beat well until light
and fluffy. Add vanilla essence.

2 Sift the dry ingredients and add,
alternately with the milk and water.

3 Whisk the egg whites with the
cream of tartar until stiff. Using a
large metal spoon, fold the egg whites
into the flour mixture.

4 Pour into two 20 cm (8 in) round,
greased and lined cake tins. Bake in
a preheated oven at 180 °C (350 °F,
gas mark 4) for 30–35 minutes. Cool
slightly in tins, then turn onto a rack.

5 For icing: beat all the ingredients
together until smooth and creamy
in consistency. Leave cake to cool
completely and sandwich with half
the icing. Ice the top of the cake with
remaining icing.

MAKES 1 LARGE CAKE

VARIATIONS
Passion fruit cake: Add 2 tbsp
passion fruit pulp to cake mixture
and another 2 tbsp to the icing.
Orange cake: Substitute milk and
water with orange juice. Omit the
vanilla essence and add 1 tsp
grated orange rind.
Nut cake: Add 75 g (2½ oz)
chopped walnuts to mixture.
Spice cake: Sift 1 tsp ground
cinnamon, 1 tsp ground ginger
and scant ½ tsp ground cloves with
dry ingredients. Omit essence.
Chocolate cake: Mix 25 g (scant
1 oz) cocoa powder with 3 tbsp
lukewarm milk and add to mixture.

CARROT CAKE

200 ml (7 fl oz) corn or sunflower oil
250 g (8½ oz) light brown sugar
185 g (6½ oz) plain flour
1½ tsp baking powder
½ tsp bicarbonate of soda
2 tsp ground cinnamon
1 tsp ground ginger
scant ½ tsp salt
3 large eggs, beaten
300 g (10½ oz) grated carrots
75 g (2½ oz) chopped pecan nuts
(optional)

CREAM CHEESE ICING
50 g (1¾ oz) butter or margarine,
softened
325 g (11 oz) icing sugar
1 tsp vanilla essence
100 g (3½ oz) sieved cottage cheese

1 Beat together oil and sugar. Sift dry
ingredients and add half to oil-sugar
mixture. Mix well. Add remaining dry
ingredients, alternately with eggs.

2 Add carrots and nuts (if using)
and mix well. Spoon into a greased
23 cm (9 in) loose-bottomed round tin
or a 22 cm (8¾ in) ring tin.

3 Bake in a preheated oven at 180 °C
(350 °F, gas mark 4) for 50-60 minutes.
Leave to cool slightly in tin before
turning onto a rack to cool completely.

4 For icing: cream butter, then add
icing sugar and remaining ingredients.
Mix until blended; do not overmix as it
will become runny. Spread on top of
cake and decorate with extra chopped
nuts if desired.

MAKES 1 LARGE CAKE

Clockwise from top left: *Peanut Butter Loaf, Carrot Cake, Butter Cake.*

MOIST DARK CHOCOLATE CAKE

125 g (4½ oz) butter
200 g (7 oz) caster sugar
3 large eggs
2 tbsp smooth apricot jam
250 ml (8½ fl oz) boiling water
2 tsp instant coffee powder
225 g (8 oz) plain flour
3 tbsp cocoa powder
1 tsp baking powder
2 tsp bicarbonate of soda
pinch of salt

BUTTER ICING
125 g (4½ oz) butter
200 g (7 oz) icing sugar
3 tbsp cocoa powder
1 tsp vanilla essence
1 tbsp milk, if required

1 Cream butter and sugar. Add eggs, one at a time, beating well after each addition until light and fluffy. Add apricot jam.

2 Add boiling water to coffee powder and leave to cool slightly.

3 Sift dry ingredients and add, alternately with coffee, to egg mixture. Turn into two lined, greased 20 cm (8 in) round cake tins. Bake in a preheated oven at 180 °C (350 °F, gas mark 4) for 20–25 minutes. Cool slightly in tins before turning out onto a rack.

4 For icing: beat all the ingredients until smooth and creamy. Sandwich cakes with half the icing, then ice the top with remaining icing.

MAKES 1 LARGE CAKE

ULTIMATE CHEESECAKE

PASTRY
125 g (4½ oz) plain flour
scant ½ tsp baking powder
3 tbsp caster sugar
80 g (2¾ oz) butter or margarine
1 tsp grated lemon rind
scant ½ tsp vanilla essence
1 large egg yolk

FILLING
1 kg (2¼ lb) sieved cottage cheese
250 ml (8½ fl oz) soured cream
140 g (5 oz) caster sugar
30 g (1 oz) plain flour
3 large eggs
1 tsp vanilla essence
1 tsp grated lemon rind

TOPPING
110 g (4 oz) granadilla or passion
fruit pulp
2 tbsp caster sugar
4 tbsp orange juice
about 1 tbsp cornflour

1 For pastry: sift flour and baking powder. Add sugar. Rub in butter with your fingertips until crumbly. Add lemon rind, essence and egg yolk. Knead lightly on floured surface. Refrigerate for at least 30 minutes.

2 Press pastry onto base and sides of a greased 23 cm (9 in) round springform tin. Bake in a preheated oven at 200 °C (400 °F, gas mark 6) for about 8 minutes. Remove from oven and cool. Reduce oven temperature to 160 °C (325 °F, gas mark 3).

3 For filling: beat together the cottage cheese, soured cream, sugar and flour until smooth.

4 Add eggs, one at a time, vanilla essence and lemon rind and mix well. Pour the filling into pastry case and bake for 1–1¼ hours, or until set. Remove from the oven.

5 For topping: combine all the ingredients in a saucepan and heat until thickened. Pour topping over filling, cool and refrigerate to set.

MAKES 1 LARGE CAKE

VARIATION
Divide filling in half and add 35 g (1¼ oz) cocoa powder to one half. Spoon the chocolate mix on top of the cheesecake before baking or swirl through.

TIP
When cheesecakes are difficult to cut, use a thin-bladed knife that has been moistened with a warm, wet towel. Push the blade length-ways into the cake and pull it straight out from the bottom. Clean and moisten the blade with the wet towel before each cut.

APRICOT-ALMOND CAKE

BASE
80 g (2¾ oz) butter or margarine
80 g (2¾ oz) caster sugar
1 large egg
155 g (5½ oz) self-raising flour

TOPPING
110 g (scant 4 oz) smooth apricot
jam
410 g can apricot halves
in syrup
100 g (3½ oz) butter
130 g (4¾ oz) caster sugar
2 large eggs
50 g (1¼ oz) self-raising flour
50 g (1¼ oz) ground almonds
2 tbsp reserved apricot syrup
scant ½ tsp almond essence
icing sugar for dusting

1 For base: cream butter and sugar. Add egg and beat until light and fluffy.

2 Sift flour. Mix into sugar mixture. Knead lightly. Press into a 23 x 32 cm (9 x 13 in) greased Swiss roll tin.

3 For topping: spread jam over base. Drain apricots, but reserve liquid. Place apricots on jam, round sides up.

4 Cream butter and caster sugar. Add eggs, one at a time, beating well until light and fluffy.

5 Sift flour and add to mixture with almonds, 2 tbsp apricot syrup and essence. Spoon over apricot halves.

6 Bake in a preheated oven at 180 °C (350 °F, gas mark 4) for 30–35 minutes. Remove from the oven and leave to cool completely in the tin. Dust with icing sugar and cut into squares.

MAKES ABOUT 30 SQUARES

VARIATION
Substitute apricot halves with any other canned fruit.

Clockwise from top: *Ultimate Cheesecake, Apricot-Almond Cake, Ultimate Cheesecake (Chocolate variation).*

MOIST BUTTERMILK CHOCOLATE CAKE

125 g (4½ oz) butter
105 g (3¾ oz) caster sugar
1 tsp vanilla essence
2 large eggs
165 g (scant 6 oz) smooth
apricot jam
155 g (5½ oz) self-raising flour
½ tsp bicarbonate of soda
50 g (1¾ oz) cocoa powder
250 ml (8½ fl oz) buttermilk

CHOCOLATE ICING
125 g (4½ oz) dark chocolate
60 g (2 oz) butter
2 tbsp cream (optional)

1 Cream butter and sugar. Add vanilla essence and eggs, one at a time, and beat until light and fluffy. Add jam and beat until smooth.

2 Sift flour, bicarbonate of soda and cocoa and add, alternately with buttermilk, to butter mixture. Mix until smooth.

3 Line a loose-bottomed round cake tin of about 22 cm (8¾ in) diameter with greaseproof paper and spoon in mixture. Bake in a preheated oven at 180 °C (350 °F, gas mark 4) for 35–40 minutes. Leave to cool slightly in the tin before turning onto a wire rack to cool.

4 For chocolate icing: combine chocolate, butter and cream in a saucepan and stir over low heat until smooth. Remove from heat and spread over cake.

MAKES 1 LARGE CAKE

MERINGUE CAKE

Serve this cake on the day of baking as it will begin to soften after it has been assembled.

BASE
125 g (4½ oz) butter or
margarine
70 g (2½ oz) caster sugar
4 large egg yolks
125 g (4½ oz) plain flour
2 tsp baking powder
scant ½ tsp salt
125 ml (4 fl oz) milk

MERINGUE
4 large egg whites
pinch of cream of tartar
160 g (5¾ oz) caster sugar
75 g (2½ oz) chopped pecan nuts
(optional)

CUSTARD
350 ml (11½ fl oz) milk
2 tbsp caster sugar
3 tbsp custard powder
1 tsp vanilla essence
125 ml (4 fl oz) double cream,
whipped (optional)

1 For base: cream butter and sugar.

2 Add the egg yolks, one at a time, and beat until light and fluffy. Sift the dry ingredients together and add, alternately with the milk, to the mixture.

3 Divide the mixture between two greased, lined 23 cm (9 in) round, loose-bottomed cake tins.

4 For meringue: whisk the egg whites until foamy. Add cream of tartar and continue to whisk.

5 Gradually whisk in the sugar until soft peaks form. Fold in the nuts. Spread the meringue over the uncooked cake mixture.

6 Bake in a preheated oven at 160 °C (325 °F, gas mark 3) for about 30 minutes, or until the meringue is golden. Allow to cool slightly in tins before removing to cool further.

7 For custard: heat milk, then add sugar and custard powder, stirring until thickened. Leave to cool, add vanilla essence and fold in the whipped cream (if using).

8 To assemble: place one cake layer, meringue side up, on a serving plate. Spread the custard over this layer and top with the remaining cake layer, meringue side up.

MAKES 1 LARGE CAKE

VARIATIONS
Instead of vanilla essence, add Van der Hum or Kirsch liqueur to the custard.
Fold whole or sliced strawberries into the cold custard and use extra strawberries to garnish.
Add 30 g (1 oz) chocolate to the hot milk to make a chocolate custard.

TIP
To easily whisk egg whites, add a few drops of fresh lemon juice.

Left to right: *Moist Buttermilk Chocolate Cake, Apple Loaf.*

APPLE LOAF

125 g (4½ oz) butter or margarine,
softened

200 g (7 oz) caster sugar

2 large eggs

1 tsp vanilla essence

250 g (8½ oz) plain flour

scant ½ tsp salt

1 tsp baking powder

½ tsp bicarbonate of soda

1 tsp ground cinnamon

scant ½ tsp grated nutmeg

125 ml (4 fl oz) milk

2 tart apples, peeled and chopped

75 g (2½ oz) chopped walnuts
or pecan nuts

1 Cream butter and sugar. Add eggs, one at a time, and essence and mix.

2 Sift together the flour, salt, baking powder, bicarbonate of soda, cinnamon and nutmeg. Gradually beat the dry ingredients, alternately with the milk, into butter mixture. Stir in apples and walnuts. Spoon into a greased 23 cm (9 in) loaf tin.

3 Bake in a preheated oven at 180 °C (350 °F, gas mark 4) for 50–60 minutes. Cool for 10 minutes in the tin. Turn onto a rack to cool.

MAKES 1 LOAF

VARIATIONS

Add 50 g (1¾ oz) chocolate chips to mixture just before baking. If you do not have any fresh apples, use a 385 g can apple pie filling instead. Alternatively, use any other fruit of choice.

BREADS

It is known that kneading bread is therapeutic. These days though, bread-making has become easy due to the availability of easy-blend yeast, which is added directly to the dry ingredients. The advantage of using easy-blend yeast is that the dough may need only one rising, and proving time may be reduced. The yeast can be stored in a cool, dry place for up to 18 months.

TYPES

Kneaded breads are made by adding enough flour to form a stiff dough that has to be kneaded, such as for rolls and pita breads. With batter breads, the ingredients are combined and beaten to make a soft, sticky dough that is not kneaded. This soft batter dough requires a container or a tin for baking.

LIQUIDS

Yeast needs warm liquid to dissolve and activate it. The liquid should feel warm on the back of your hand, ideally around 30–35 °C (86–95 °F). A guide, if no thermometer is available, is to add one-third boiling liquid to two-thirds cold. If the liquid is too cold, the dough will rise too slowly. If it is too hot, it will kill the yeast.

A loaf made with water will have a heavy, crisp crust and a chewy texture, like French breads. Milk, which is very popular for breads, gives a light, even texture and a thin brown crust, and adding fat keeps bread fresh for longer. Buttermilk and yoghurt make a fine-textured bread with a rich flavour.

MIXING

Mixing starts when warm liquid is stirred into dry ingredients containing yeast. This starts activating the yeast.

When mixing dough, it is important to know how bread should feel. Mixing by hand can take up to 10 minutes. All flours vary slightly in the amount of liquid they absorb. The amount of flour in a recipe is a guide. Because of atmospheric and technical influences, bread is unique with every mixing. Experience will later guide you.

KNEADING AND RISING (PROVING)

Lightly flour your hands. Gently bring the far edge of dough forward and fold it over. With the heel of your hand, push the dough away from you; give the dough a quarter turn and repeat. Keep folding and turning until the dough feels smooth. Kneading makes dough smooth and elastic. If dough starts to stick to your hands or to the surface, flour them. Add a little flour at first, as too much flour will result in a stiff, dry bread. When kneaded sufficiently, the dough should feel supple and elastic, and should spring back if pressed with a finger. If the dough is too soft, work in a little more flour.

Grease deep plastic containers by brushing with oil or using non-stick spray. Place the ball of dough in the container and turn it over to grease the other side. Cling film works well as a cover to keep in the moisture. Leave the dough to rise in a warm place, away from draughts, until doubled in size. It is difficult to predict an exact rising time as this depends on the temperature of the dough, the amount of yeast and general atmospheric conditions.

KNOCKING BACK AND SECOND RISING

After it has risen, knock back the dough and knead briefly until the original volume is achieved. This ensures an even texture. Shape the dough – use your imagination and form your own shapes. Once a shape is formed, try not to reshape it again. If shaped in a tin, the dough should fill half to two-thirds of the tin. Cover with cling film. Leave dough to prove until doubled in size.

Most loaves are cut with decorative slashes before they are placed in the oven so the dough will expand during baking. Do not make the slashes too deep. Glaze the dough with milk, melted butter or beaten egg for a better finish.

BAKING

Place tins in the centre of an oven preheated to 200–220 °C (400–425 °F, gas mark 6–7). Check the bread near the end of baking. When ready, it will sound hollow if you tap the bottom. Use baking times given in recipes as a guide only. If the top of the bread is browning too fast, place a piece of aluminium foil loosely over the loaf.

COOLING AND STORING

Remove bread immediately from tins and cool on wire racks before slicing.

Bread freezes well for up to three months and can be reheated or thawed in a moderate oven.

Spinach and Cheese Plait (page 48)

ITALIAN-STYLE CHEESE BREAD

385 g (13½ oz) white bread flour
1 tbsp brown sugar
scant ½ tsp salt
2 tsp easy-blend yeast
20 g (¾ oz) sun-dried tomatoes, chopped
1 tbsp chopped fresh mixed herbs or 1 tsp dried
15 black or green olives, pitted (optional)
50 g (1¾ oz) grated Cheddar cheese
about 500 ml (17 fl oz) lukewarm water
2 tbsp olive or sunflower oil

1 Sift flour, sugar and salt. Add yeast, tomatoes, herbs, olives and cheese. Add water and oil and stir well to combine.

2 Spoon mixture into a well-greased 23 cm (9 in) loaf tin. Cover and leave in a warm place until risen to the top of the tin.

3 Bake in a preheated oven at 200 °C (400 °F, gas mark 6) for 35–40 minutes. Turn out onto a wire rack to cool. Serve with butter if liked.

MAKES 1 LOAF

VARIATION
Substitute olives with 1 small chopped onion.

TIP
To pit olives easily, lay them on a board and roll over them with a heavy rolling pin.

SEEDED GRANARY BREAD

225 g (8 oz) wholemeal bread flour
210 g (7½ oz) granary flour
1 tsp salt
2 tsp easy-blend yeast
2 tbsp sunflower seeds
1 tbsp sesame seeds
about 375 ml (12½ fl oz) lukewarm water
1 tbsp honey or golden syrup
1 tbsp sunflower oil

1 Mix flours and salt together. Add yeast and seeds.

2 Add water, honey and oil and mix into dry ingredients to make a moist dough.

3 Mix well and spoon into a well-greased 23 cm (9 in) loaf tin. Cover and allow to rise in a warm place to double in size.

4 Bake in a preheated oven at 180 °C (350 °F, gas mark 4) for 40–45 minutes. Bake mini loaves for about 30 minutes. Turn out onto a wire rack to cool.

MAKES 1 LOAF

TIP
To test if bread is baked, remove it from the tin, turn it upside down and tap the underside. If it is ready, it should sound hollow, like a drum. If it sounds heavy or dense, return it to the oven to bake for a few more minutes.

SPINACH AND CHEESE PLAIT

30 g (1 oz) butter
1 small onion, chopped
150 g (5½ oz) fresh spinach, chopped
2 tsp chopped fresh thyme or ½ tsp dried
freshly ground black pepper to taste
315 g (10¾ oz) self-raising flour
scant ½ tsp salt
50 g (1¾ oz) finely grated Cheddar cheese
50 g (1¾ oz) feta cheese, crumbled
about 200 ml (7 fl oz) milk

1 Heat butter in a heavy-based pan and sauté onion until soft. Add spinach and cook for a few minutes, stirring, until soft. Add thyme and pepper, remove from heat to cool, then drain off excess water.

2 Sift flour and salt. Stir in Cheddar cheese and half the feta. Add spinach mixture and enough milk to mix into a soft dough.

3 Turn dough onto a lightly floured surface and knead lightly until smooth. Divide dough into three long pieces. Plait together on a greased baking tray. Sprinkle with remaining feta cheese.

4 Bake in a preheated oven at 180 °C (350 °F, gas mark 4) for 40–45 minutes. This bread can be served warm or cold.

MAKES 1 LARGE BREAD

Left to right: *Seeded Granary Bread (various shapes), Italian-style Cheese Bread.*

PITA BREADS

Use pita breads as a base for pizzas.
Simply add toppings of choice.

420 g (15 oz) white bread flour
1 tsp salt
1 tsp caster sugar
2 tsp easy-blend yeast
125 ml (4 fl oz) warm milk
125 ml (4 fl oz) plain yoghurt
1 large egg, lightly beaten
4 tbsp lukewarm water
1 tbsp sunflower oil

1 Sift flour and salt. Add sugar and mix. Add yeast.

2 Whisk remaining ingredients together and mix into dry ingredients. Turn dough onto a lightly floured surface and knead until smooth and elastic. Cover and leave to rise in a warm place until doubled in size.

3 Turn dough onto a lightly floured surface and knead until smooth. Divide dough into eight equal portions. Knead each portion into a ball, and press into 20 cm (8 in) rounds with the palm of your hand.

4 Place on lightly floured baking trays, leaving enough space in between to rise. Leave to prove in a warm place until risen.

5 Bake in a preheated oven at 190 °C (375 °F, gas mark 5) for about 10 minutes or until bread is lightly browned and the rounds have puffed.

MAKES 8 BREADS

BASIL AND PEPPER CORNBREAD SLICES

125 g (4½ oz) butter
1 onion, chopped
1 red pepper, seeded and chopped
225 g (8 oz) cornmeal (maize meal) or polenta
155 g (5½ oz) plain flour
50 g (1¾ oz) caster sugar
1 tbsp baking powder
1½ tsp salt
½ tsp bicarbonate of soda
pinch of cayenne pepper
375 ml (12½ fl oz) buttermilk
3 large eggs
60 g (2 oz) grated mozzarella cheese
410 g can sweetcorn kernels, drained
3 tbsp chopped fresh basil or 1 tbsp dried

1 Melt 25 g (scant 1 oz) butter in a medium saucepan and sauté onion and red pepper until soft. Set aside.

2 Sift dry ingredients into a large bowl. Add remaining butter and rub in with fingertips until mixture resembles coarse breadcrumbs.

3 Whisk buttermilk and eggs and add to dry mixture. Add cheese, sweetcorn, pepper mixture and basil. Mix well.

4 Spoon into a greased 24 x 34 cm (10 x 14 in) baking tin. Bake in a preheated oven at 200 °C (400 °F, gas mark 6) for 20–25 minutes until golden. Leave to cool in the tin, then cut into fingers or squares.

MAKES ABOUT 28 FINGERS

SPRING ONION AND GARLIC ROLLS

560 g (1¼ lb) white bread flour
2 tsp salt
2 tsp caster sugar
2 tsp easy-blend yeast
4 tbsp chopped spring onions
4 cloves garlic, crushed
about 375 ml (12½ fl oz) lukewarm water
2 tbsp sunflower oil
30 g (1 oz) butter or margarine, melted

1 Sift flour and salt. Add sugar and mix. Add yeast, spring onions and crushed garlic. Add water and oil to dry ingredients to make a soft dough.

2 Knead on a lightly floured surface until dough is smooth and elastic. Cover and leave to rise in a warm place until doubled in size. Knead again and divide dough into 12 pieces. Roll each piece into a bun shape.

3 Brush rolls with melted butter and leave to prove. Bake in a preheated oven at 180 °C (350 °F, gas mark 4) for 20–25 minutes.

MAKES 12 ROLLS

VARIATION
Substitute fresh garlic with 1 tsp dried garlic flakes.

TIP
Easy-blend yeast is easy to use. Sold in most supermarkets, it can be stored for up to 18 months at room temperature.

Clockwise from left: *Spring Onion and Garlic Rolls, Pita Breads, Basil and Pepper Cornbread Slices.*

HONEY OAT BREAD

420 g (15 oz) white or brown
bread flour
1 tsp salt
80 g (2¼ oz) rolled oats
2 tsp easy-blend yeast
1 tbsp sunflower oil
65 g (2¼ oz) honey
about 375 ml (12½ fl oz)
lukewarm water

1 Sift flour and salt. Add oats and mix. Add yeast.

2 Add oil and honey to water and mix into dry ingredients. Spoon into a well-greased 23 cm (9 in) loaf tin. Cover and allow to rise in a warm place until doubled in size.

3 Bake in a preheated oven at 180 °C (350 °F, gas mark 4) for 50–60 minutes. Turn out onto a wire rack to cool.

MAKES 1 LOAF

CARAMEL-PECAN BUNS

420 g (15 oz) white bread flour
1½ tsp salt
50 g (1¾ oz) caster sugar
2 tsp easy-blend yeast
200 ml (7 fl oz) warm milk
200 ml (7 fl oz) warm water
3 tbsp sunflower oil

FILLING
60 g (2 oz) butter or margarine
50 g (1¾ oz) caster sugar
1 tbsp ground cinnamon
35 g (1¼ oz) coarsely chopped
pecans for topping

1 Sift flour and salt. Add sugar and mix. Add yeast.

2 Add milk, water and oil to the dry ingredients and mix to form a soft dough.

3 Turn onto a lightly floured surface and knead until the dough is smooth and elastic.

4 Place in a greased or oiled bowl, cover and leave it to rise in a warm place until doubled in size.

5 Knock back dough. Turn onto a lightly floured surface and roll out into a rectangular shape of about 35 x 27 cm (14 x 11 in).

6 For filling: melt half the butter and brush over surface of dough. Combine sugar and cinnamon and sprinkle over the brushed butter. Roll up like a Swiss roll, starting from the long side, then cut into 12–15 slices.

7 Melt remaining butter and brush it over the slices. Sprinkle nuts over. Place rolls, cut side down, on a greased baking tray. Cover and leave to prove. Bake in a preheated oven at 200 °C (400 °F, gas mark 6) for 15–20 minutes, or until light brown.

MAKES 12–15

TIP
To test whether the dough has risen properly, try gently pressing with your finger. If the dough is ready, it should spring back.

POT BREAD

1 kg (2¼ lb) white bread flour
2 tsp salt
2 tsp caster sugar
2 tsp easy-blend yeast
60 g (2 oz) butter or margarine
about 650 ml (1 pint 2 fl oz)
lukewarm water

1 Sift flour and salt. Add sugar and mix. Add yeast.

2 Rub butter into dry ingredients and gradually add water to mix to a soft dough. Add more water if necessary.

3 Turn out onto a floured surface and knead dough until smooth and elastic. Place dough in an oiled bowl, cover and leave to rise until doubled in size.

4 Knock back the dough and divide it in two. Place each portion in a greased round tin or a heavy-based ovenproof pot, cover and leave to prove in a warm place until doubled in size.

5 Brush the tops with water or milk and bake in preheated oven at 200 °C (400 °F, gas mark 6) for 45–50 minutes.

MAKES 2 ROUND BREADS

VARIATION
Roosterkoek: Follow recipe for pot bread, but divide dough into about 36 pieces and cook on a grid over coals, or in a griddle pan on the cooker.

Clockwise from top left: *Pot Bread, Honey Oat Bread, Roosterkoek (Pot Bread variation), Caramel-Pecan Buns.*

SOFT ROLLS

560 g (1¼ lb) white bread flour
1 tsp salt
4 tsp caster sugar
4 tsp milk powder or coffee creamer
2 tsp easy-blend yeast
30 g (1 oz) butter or margarine
about 250 ml (8½ fl oz)
lukewarm water
beaten egg or milk to glaze
sesame seeds, poppy seeds
or grated cheese for topping

1 Sift flour and salt. Add sugar and milk powder and mix. Add yeast.

2 Rub butter into dry ingredients with your fingertips until mixture resembles fine breadcrumbs.

3 Add just enough water to mix to a soft dough. Turn onto a lightly floured surface and knead for about 10 minutes until the dough is smooth and elastic.

4 Place dough in an oiled bowl, cover and leave to rise until doubled in size.

5 Knock back dough and divide into 15 equal pieces. Roll each piece into a ball, or shape into long sausages.

6 Using a rolling pin, roll each ball or sausage of dough into a long oval and roll up tightly, like a Swiss roll. Place bread rolls, with seam at bottom, on a greased baking tray.

7 Cover the tray with oiled cling film and leave to prove in a warm place until doubled in size.

8 Brush with beaten egg or milk and sprinkle with sesame seeds, poppy seeds or grated cheese.

9 Bake in a preheated oven at 200 °C (400 °F, gas mark 6) for 15–20 minutes.

MAKES 15

VARIATION
Plaited bread
1. Follow recipe for soft rolls. After rising the first time, knock back dough and divide into three equal pieces.
2. Roll each piece into a 40 cm (16 in) long strand.
3. Plait the three strands until all the dough has been used. Seal ends together well. Leave to prove in a warm place until doubled in size. Brush with beaten egg or milk and sprinkle with poppy seeds.
4. Bake in a preheated oven at 200 °C (400 °F, gas mark 6) for 20–25 minutes. Bake mini breads for 15–20 minutes.

TIP
The dough will be sticky when you start kneading, but will become smooth and silky quite quickly. To knead, stretch the dough away from you with the heel of your hand, then turn and repeat the movement. Dough is sufficiently kneaded when the impression of a finger springs back.

SPICY FRUIT BREAD

150 g (5½ oz) mixed dried fruit
4 tbsp rum
560 g (1¼ lb) white bread flour
1½ tsp salt
2½ tsp mixed spice
3 tbsp caster sugar
2 tsp easy-blend yeast
about 300 ml (10 fl oz)
lukewarm water
2 tbsp melted butter or
sunflower oil

SUGAR GLAZE
80 ml (2¾ fl oz) water
2 tbsp caster sugar

1 Soak cake mix in rum for about 1 hour. Drain.

2 Sift the flour, salt and spice. Add sugar and mix. Add yeast. Add the soaked fruit, water and butter and mix to form a dough.

3 Knead dough until it is smooth and elastic. Shape into a roll to fit into a lightly greased 23 cm (9 in) loaf tin.

4 Cover and leave to rise in a warm place until doubled in size. Bake in a preheated oven at 180 °C (350 °F, gas mark 4) for 30–35 minutes until golden brown.

5 For glaze: heat water and sugar over moderate heat until sugar has dissolved and brush over hot bread.

MAKES 1 LOAF

VARIATION
Substitute rum with strained tea.

Clockwise from top: *Spicy Fruit Bread, Soft Rolls, Plaited Mini Bread.*

YOGHURT BREAD

300 g (10½ oz) wholemeal flour
280 g (10 oz) cracked wheat
1 tsp salt
1 tsp bicarbonate of soda
2 tbsp honey
625 ml (1 pint + 2 tbsp) plain
yoghurt or buttermilk

1 Sift flour. Add bran left in sieve
and add all the other ingredients.
Mix well.

2 Spoon into a greased 23 cm (9 in)
loaf tin. Sprinkle extra crushed wheat
over the top.

3 Bake in a preheated oven at 180 °C
(350 °F, gas mark 4) for 45–50 minutes.
Turn out onto a wire rack to cool.

MAKES 1 LOAF

VARIATION
To make a seed bread: add
3 tbsp poppyseeds.

TOMATO AND ONION COTTAGE BREAD

FILLING
1 tbsp olive oil
1 medium onion, chopped
1 clove garlic, crushed
3 medium tomatoes,
skinned and chopped
1 tbsp chopped fresh oregano
or 1 tsp dried
salt and freshly ground black
pepper to taste

BREAD
420 g (15 oz) white bread flour
1½ tsp salt
1 tbsp caster sugar
2 tsp easy-blend yeast
1 tbsp olive oil
about 200 ml (7 fl oz) warm milk

1 For filling: heat oil in a heavy-
based saucepan. Add onion and garlic
and sauté until soft.

2 Add tomatoes, oregano and
seasoning. Simmer for 10 minutes
or until tomatoes have softened and
most of the liquid has evaporated.
Leave to cool slightly.

3 For bread: sift flour and salt into a
bowl. Add sugar, yeast and one-third
of tomato filling. Mix. Add oil and
enough milk to mix to a soft dough.

4 Knead dough on a lightly floured
surface until smooth and elastic. Place
dough in an oiled bowl, cover and
leave to rise in a warm place until
doubled in size.

5 Turn dough onto a lightly floured
surface and knead until smooth.
Shape into a round and place on
a greased baking tray. Cut a large
cross in the top of the round and
fill with remaining tomato filling.
Leave to prove in a warm place to
double in size.

6 Bake in a preheated oven at 180 °C
(350 °F, gas mark 4) for 40–45 minutes,
or until loaf sounds hollow when
tapped on base.

MAKES 1 LARGE ROUND BREAD

MEALIE BREAD

125 g (4½ oz) butter or margarine,
melted
75 g (2½ oz) caster sugar
3 large eggs
280 g (10 oz) white bread flour
1 tbsp baking powder
½ tsp salt
80 g (2¾ oz) cornmeal (maize meal)
or polenta
410 g can cream-style sweetcorn
125 ml (4 fl oz) milk

1 Cream butter and sugar. Add
eggs, one at a time, and beat until
light and fluffy.

2 Sift flour, baking powder and
salt and add to butter mixture. Add
cornmeal, sweetcorn and milk and
mix well. Spoon mixture into a greased
23 cm (9 in) loaf tin and bake in a
preheated oven at 180 °C (350 °F,
gas mark 4) for 50–55 minutes. Turn
out onto a wire rack to cool.

MAKES 1 LOAF

VARIATIONS
Substitute the cream-style
sweetcorn with a can of
sweetcorn kernels, drained.
Bake in any other containers for
interesting shapes and sizes.

Clockwise from top left: *Ciabatta Roll, Tomato and Onion Cottage Bread, Mealie Bread, Yoghurt Bread.*

CIABATTA ROLLS

700 g (1 lb 9 oz) white bread flour
2 tsp salt
1 tsp caster sugar
2 tsp easy-blend yeast
2 tbsp milk
2 tbsp olive oil
about 450 ml (15 fl oz)
warm water

1 Sift flour and salt. Add sugar and mix. Add yeast. Stir in milk, olive oil and enough water to make a soft dough.

2 Knead dough until it becomes smooth and elastic. Cover dough with oiled cling film and leave to rise in a warm place until doubled in size.

3 Knock back and divide into six pieces. Shape into ovals and make deep indentations in each roll. Sprinkle with flour, cover and leave in a warm place until doubled in size.

4 Bake in a preheated oven at 200 °C (400 °F, gas mark 6) for 20–25 minutes.

MAKES 6 LARGE ROLLS

SWEET TARTS AND FLANS

With the exception of choux pastry, uncooked pastry dough will keep, well wrapped in cling film, in the refrigerator for 2–3 days. Raw pastry dough can be frozen, but it must be allowed to defrost completely before attempting to roll it out, or it may crack. In most cases, pastry can be shaped and frozen before baking, then baked straight from the freezer quite successfully. The secret of successful pastry making lies in accurate measuring, using the correct proportions of fat to flour and careful handling. Choux pastry is the exception, as all other pastries need to be kept cool. Pastry must rest beforehand, or it will shrink during baking. Most pastries should be allowed to rest in the refrigerator, well wrapped in cling film. Where a recipe specifies the weight of pastry, this generally refers to the weight of the flour and not the combined weight of all the ingredients. When buying ready-made pastry, however, the weight specified on the packet is the combined weight of the ingredients.

PASTRY INGREDIENTS

For most pastries, plain flour is used for a light, crisp result. Self-raising flour will produce a soft, spongy pastry. Wholemeal flour gives heavier dough, which is more difficult to roll. For wholemeal pastry use half wholemeal and half white flour.

Take care when adding the liquid to dough. Too much will result in a tough end result. Use chilled water and add just enough to bind the dough. Egg yolks are used to enrich pastry.

MIXING

For most pastries, cold butter has to be rubbed into the flour. The butter is cut into small pieces, then added to the flour. Then, using your fingertips, lightly take small amounts of the mixture and rub into tiny pieces to resemble fine crumbs.

When adding the liquid, sprinkle this evenly over the surface. Don't add all the liquid at once as the amount needed will be determined by the absorbency of the flour. Knead dough lightly for a few seconds.

When using a food processor, first place the flour in the processor, add the butter and blend for a few seconds. Gradually add water until the dough is just beginning to hold together.

ROLLING OUT PASTRY

A cool surface, such as marble, is ideal for rolling out pastry. Dust the work surface and rolling pin, never the pastry, very lightly with flour. Roll the dough lightly and evenly in one direction only, until thin. The usual thickness for rolling out pastries is 3 mm (⅛ in) – puff pastry is sometimes rolled out to 5 mm (¼ in).

SHAPING PASTRY

Pastry is most often used to line flan and tart tins and to cover pies. Pastry can also be folded around fillings or wrapped around whole boned fish or meat.

BAKING BLIND

This is when you prebake pastry before adding a filling. Prick the base with a fork, then line with a large piece of greaseproof paper. Fill with dried beans and bake for 10–15 minutes at a high temperature or until pastry looks set. Remove beans and bake for a further 5 minutes until the pastry is firm and lightly coloured.

GLAZING

Glazing pastry seals the surface and gives a golden brown appearance. Brush lightly with egg yolk beaten with a little water, or use milk.

GREEK COCONUT TART

60 g (2 oz) butter or margarine
65 g (2¼ oz) caster sugar
2 large eggs
60 g (2 oz) plain flour
scant ½ tsp baking powder
pinch of salt
80 g (2¾ oz) desiccated coconut
125 ml (4 fl oz) milk

SYRUP
100 g (3½ oz) granulated sugar
125 ml (4 fl oz) water
1 tsp vanilla essence

1 Cream butter and sugar. Add eggs, one at a time, and beat well until light and fluffy. Sift flour, baking powder and salt and add to butter mixture with the coconut.

2 Add milk, mix and pour into a greased 23 cm (9 in) pie plate. Bake in a preheated oven at 160 °C (325 °F, gas mark 3) for 35–40 minutes until golden brown.

3 For syrup: boil all ingredients together until sugar has dissolved. Pour syrup over hot tart.

MAKES 1 TART

Almond-Pear Flan (page 60)

CRUSTLESS COCONUT MILK TART

85 g (3 oz) plain flour
450 ml (15 fl oz) milk
150 g (5½ oz) caster sugar
60 g (2 oz) desiccated coconut
50 g (1¼ oz) butter or margarine, melted
3 large eggs
1 tsp vanilla essence
scant ½ tsp baking powder
pinch of salt

1 Sift flour and add all remaining ingredients. Mix well. Spoon into a greased 23 cm (9 in) pie plate. Bake in a preheated oven at 180 °C (350 °F, gas mark 4) for 40–45 minutes until light brown. Leave to cool.

MAKES 1 TART

ALMOND-PEAR FLAN

PASTRY
85 g (3 oz) plain flour
scant ½ tsp salt
60 g (2 oz) butter
70 g (2½ oz) caster sugar
2 large egg yolks
scant ½ tsp vanilla essence

FILLING
1 large egg
1 large egg yolk
100 g (3½ oz) caster sugar
30 g (1 oz) plain flour
250 ml (8½ fl oz) milk
45 g (1½ oz) butter or margarine
1 tsp almond essence
25 g (scant 1 oz) ground almonds
410 g can pear halves, drained
85 g (3 oz) smooth apricot jam

1 For pastry: sift flour and salt together. Rub in butter until the mixture resembles breadcrumbs.

2 Add sugar, egg yolks and vanilla essence. Mix well, wrap airtight and refrigerate for about 30 minutes.

3 Roll out pastry on a lightly floured surface and use to line a greased 24 cm (9½ in) loose-bottomed flan tin. Prick the base with a fork, line with grease-proof paper and fill with dried beans.

4 Bake blind in a preheated oven at 190 °C (375 °F, gas mark 5) for about 10 minutes. Remove from oven. Remove paper and beans.

5 For filling: beat egg, egg yolk and sugar until light and fluffy. Sift flour and add to mixture with the milk, beating well. Place in heavy-based saucepan and heat until thickened, about 2–3 minutes.

6 Remove from heat and add butter, almond essence and almonds. Set aside to cool slightly.

7 Fill case with filling and arrange pears on top. Heat jam and brush over the top of the tart and over the pears. Bake in preheated oven at 180 °C (350 °F, gas mark 4) for 15–20 minutes. Cut into wedges to serve.

MAKES 1 FLAN

TIP
Freeze any leftover egg whites, remembering to mark the exact number and date on the freezer bag or sticker.

APPLE TART

2 large eggs
150 g (5½ oz) caster sugar
80 g (2¾ oz) butter or margarine, melted
4 tbsp milk
125 g (4½ oz) self-raising flour
2 large tart apples, peeled and chopped or sliced

SAUCE
165 g can evaporated milk
100 g (3½ oz) granulated sugar
2 tsp caramel essence

1 Beat eggs and sugar until creamy. Add melted butter. Add milk. Sift flour and add.

2 Add apples and pour the mixture into a greased 22 cm (9 in) square ovenproof dish.

3 Bake in a preheated oven at 180 °C (350 °F, gas mark 4) for 30–40 minutes.

4 For sauce: boil milk and sugar over low heat, stirring continuously. Remove from the heat and add caramel essence. Pour the hot sauce over the hot tart. Serve hot or cold.

MAKES 1 TART

TIP
Sprinkle lemon juice over fresh sliced apple to prevent the apple from discoloring.

Left to right: *Crustless Coconut Milk Tart, Apple Tart.*

APPLE CUSTARD FLAN

PASTRY
125 g (4½ oz) plain flour
30 g (1 oz) cornflour
scant ½ tsp salt
120 g (4¼ oz) unsalted butter,
cut into small pieces
about 1 tbsp cold water

FILLING
250 ml (8½ fl oz) double cream
3 large egg yolks
100 g (3½ oz) caster sugar
2 tbsp plain flour
1 tsp vanilla essence

TOPPING
3 medium tart apples
110 g (3¾ oz) smooth apricot jam

1 For pastry: sift flour, cornflour and salt together. Rub in butter until mixture resembles fine crumbs. Add cold water and mix to a firm dough.

2 Cover pastry and refrigerate for about 30 minutes.

3 Roll out pastry on a lightly floured surface and use to line a greased 24 cm (9½ in) loose-bottomed flan tin. Prick base with a fork, line with greaseproof paper and fill with dried beans. Bake blind in a preheated oven at 190 °C (375 °F, gas mark 5) for 10 minutes.

4 Remove from oven. Remove paper and beans. Reduce oven temperature to 180 °C (350 °F, gas mark 4).

5 For filling: heat the cream in a heavy-based saucepan. Whisk the egg yolk, sugar and flour together and pour some cream into eggs, whisking all the time. Add egg mixture to pan and heat slowly, whisking all the time until it thickens. Remove from heat, add vanilla essence and mix. Cool slightly and spoon into pastry case.

6 For topping: peel, core and slice the apples. Arrange on top of custard filling. Heat jam and brush apple slices.

7 Bake for 30–35 minutes until the apples are just tender and light golden brown. Cut into wedges to serve.

MAKES 1 FLAN

TIP
Sprinkle apples with cornflour to prevent discoloration.

GREEN FIG TART

SHORTBREAD
125 g (4½ oz) plain flour
30 g (1 oz) cornflour
65 g (2¼ oz) caster sugar
scant ½ tsp salt
125 g (4½ oz) butter
1 tsp vanilla essence

FILLING
410 g can evaporated milk
3 large eggs, separated
100 g (3½ oz) caster sugar
1 tsp vanilla essence
2 tsp gelatine
2 tbsp cold water
50 g (1¾ oz) red glacé cherries, chopped
140 g (5 oz) whole figs in syrup, drained and roughly chopped
75 g (2½ oz) chopped pecan nuts

1 For shortbread: sift dry ingredients. Rub in butter, add vanilla essence and mix to form a soft dough.

2 Press pastry into a greased 23 cm (9 in) pie plate and prick with a fork. Refrigerate for 30 minutes to firm.

3 Bake in a preheated oven at 160 °C (325 °F, gas mark 3) for 30 minutes.

4 For filling: heat evaporated milk, egg yolks and sugar in a heavy-based saucepan. Beat constantly until the custard thickens. Remove from heat and add vanilla essence.

5 Sponge gelatine in cold water. Place in container over hot water and leave until melted. Add to custard mixture.

6 Whisk egg whites until soft peaks form and add to custard mix. Add cherries, figs and nuts and mix all together. Spoon into pastry case and refrigerate until set.

MAKES 1 TART

TIP
Never boil gelatine. Sponge by mixing it into cold water and dissolve over warm water.

Top to bottom: *Green Fig Tart, Apple Custard Flan.*

QUICK MILK TART

PASTRY
125 g (4½ oz) plain flour
1 tsp baking powder
pinch of salt
65 g (2¼ oz) caster sugar
100 g (3½ oz) butter
1 large egg, beaten

FILLING
750 ml (1¼ pints) milk
80 g (2¾ oz) butter
40 g (1¼ oz) plain flour
pinch of salt
4 large eggs, separated
75 g (2½ oz) caster sugar
1 tsp vanilla essence
ground cinnamon for sprinkling

1 For pastry: sift flour, baking powder and salt. Add sugar. Rub in butter. Add beaten egg, mix well and press dough into two greased 23 cm (9 in) pie plates.

2 For filling: heat milk in a heavy-based saucepan and add butter.

3 Sift flour and salt, add egg yolks and sugar and beat well.

4 Add some boiled milk to the egg mixture, stir and pour back into pan. Boil for a few minutes until thick, stirring constantly, and remove from heat. Add vanilla essence.

5 Beat egg whites until soft peaks form and fold lightly into the cooked mixture. Pour filling into cases and sprinkle cinnamon over the top. Bake in a preheated oven at 180 °C (350 °F, gas mark 4) for 20 minutes.

MAKES 2 TARTS

CARAMEL-PEPPERMINT TART

COCONUT CASE
80 g (2¾ oz) butter
52 g (2 oz) caster sugar
60 g (2 oz) plain flour
scant ½ tsp salt
20 g (¾ oz) desiccated coconut

FILLING
1 tbsp gelatine
3 tbsp cold water
380 g can or jar caramel or
toffee sauce
50 g (1¾ oz) peppermint crisp or
chocolate mint bar, grated
250 ml (8½ fl oz) double cream,
whipped

1 For case: cream butter and sugar together. Sift flour and salt and add to butter mixture with the coconut. Press into a greased 23 cm (9 in) pie plate. Bake in a preheated oven at 180 °C (350 °F, gas mark 4) for 10–12 minutes.

2 For filling: sponge gelatine in water and dissolve over hot water. Mix remaining filling ingredients and pour into case. Refrigerate until set.

MAKES 1 TART

MANGO AND PASSION FRUIT FLAN

ALMOND CASE
80 g (2¾ oz) butter
52 g (2 oz) caster sugar
1 large egg yolk
100 g (3½ oz) plain flour
scant ½ tsp salt
50 g (1¾ oz) ground almonds

FILLING
1 tbsp gelatine
3 tbsp water
425 g can sliced mangoes
in light syrup
1 large egg white
175 ml (6 fl oz) passion fruit or
mango yoghurt
2 tbsp honey
125 ml (4 fl oz) double cream,
whipped

1 For base: cream butter and sugar. Add egg yolk and beat until light and fluffy. Sift flour and add to butter mixture with the salt and almonds. Mix to form a soft dough and press into the bottom and sides of a greased 24 cm (9½ in) loose-bottomed flan tin.

2 Bake in preheated oven at 180 °C (350 °F, gas mark 4) for 12–15 minutes until golden brown.

3 For filling: sponge gelatine in water. Place in container over hot water until melted.

4 Drain the mango syrup into a bowl, add gelatine and cool. Purée the mangoes and add.

5 Whisk the egg white until soft peaks form.

6 Combine the mango mixture, yoghurt and honey and refrigerate. When the mixture begins to set, fold in the whisked egg white and cream and pour into the cooled case.

7 Set in the refrigerator. Decorate with fruit and extra whipped cream.

MAKES 1 FLAN

Clockwise from top left: *Caramel-Peppermint Tart, Quick Milk Tart, Mango and Granadilla Flan.*

65
SWEET TARTS AND FLANS

MUFFINS AND SCONES

MUFFINS

Muffins can be sweet or savoury. Your imagination is the limit to what you can create. Most muffins are quick and easy to make and are absolutely irresistible when served, with or without butter, straight from the oven! They usually taste best on the day they are baked.

Mixing

A muffin mixture should be handled lightly. The liquid should always be mixed into the dry ingredients, stirring until just combined and moist. The batter should be lumpy. Over-mixing will result in coarse muffins, rising with peaks and tunnels.

The muffin recipes in this chapter were all tested using a 12-cup American-style muffin tray (each cup measuring about 7.5 cm/3 in across the top and 4 cm/1½ in deep). Other sizes are available and can be used. Just adjust the timing. Grease the cups with a non-stick spray or brush lightly with oil or melted butter.

Cooling

Muffins are normally baked at a moderate to high temperature. They are ready when they have risen, are browned and are firm to the touch. Use a metal skewer to check; the skewer should come out clean. Muffins will naturally have cracks on top. Turn muffins onto a wire rack to cool.

Freezing

To freeze muffins successfully for up to three months, wait for them to cool, then place in airtight freezer bags. To thaw quickly, remove from freezer bag and wrap in foil. Place in a moderate oven for 20 minutes. Alternatively, place each frozen muffin on a piece of kitchen paper in a microwave on high for 45 seconds. Microwave ovens vary in power, so take care not to overheat.

BANANA-CINNAMON MUFFINS

250 g (8½ oz) plain flour
1 tsp bicarbonate of soda
1 tsp baking powder
1 tsp ground cinnamon
scant ½ tsp salt
150 g (5½ oz) caster sugar
1 large egg, lightly beaten
80 g (2¾ oz) butter, melted
4 tbsp milk
3 large ripe bananas, mashed

1 Sift flour, bicarbonate of soda, baking powder, cinnamon and salt.

2 In another bowl, whisk sugar, egg, melted butter and milk. Add banana and stir this mixture into the flour mixture until moistened; the batter should still be lumpy.

3 Spoon the mixture into greased muffin cups, filling each one to two-thirds full.

4 Bake in a preheated oven at 200 °C (400 °F, gas mark 6) for about 20 minutes, or until golden brown. Turn out onto a wire rack to cool.

MAKES 12

CHEESE, PEPPER AND MUSHROOM MUFFINS

250 g (8½ oz) plain flour
1 tbsp baking powder
scant ½ tsp salt
pinch of ground cayenne pepper
125 g (4½ oz) button mushrooms, chopped
2 tbsp chopped spring onion
100 g (3½ oz) grated Cheddar cheese
1 red pepper, seeded and chopped
1 tbsp chopped fresh parsley
pinch of freshly ground black pepper
2 large eggs
100 ml (3½ fl oz) sunflower oil
300 ml (10 fl oz) milk
cayenne pepper for topping

1 Sift flour, baking powder, salt and cayenne pepper. Add mushrooms, spring onion, cheese, red pepper, parsley and black pepper.

2 In another bowl, whisk eggs, oil and milk. Add to dry ingredients, mixing until just combined. Spoon into greased muffin cups, filling to two-thirds full.

3 Bake in a preheated oven at 200 °C (400 °F, gas mark 6) for 15–20 minutes. Serve warm with butter.

MAKES 12

VARIATION
Ham and tomato muffins: Omit mushrooms and add 60 g (2 oz) chopped ham and 40 g (1¼ oz) chopped sun-dried tomatoes.

Cheese, Pepper and Mushroom Muffins

BEST-EVER BLUEBERRY MUFFINS

250 g (8½ oz) plain flour
2 tsp baking powder
scant ½ tsp salt
150 g (5½ oz) caster sugar
100 ml (3½ fl oz) sunflower oil
2 large eggs
100 ml (3½ fl oz) milk
400 g (14 oz) fresh blueberries

1 Sift flour, baking powder and salt together. Add sugar.

2 In another bowl, whisk oil, eggs and milk and add to flour mixture.

3 Fold blueberries into mixture; batter should still be lumpy. Spoon mixture into greased muffin cups, filling each to two-thirds full.

4 Bake in a preheated oven at 200 °C (400 °F, gas mark 6) for 20–25 minutes, or until golden brown. Turn out onto a wire rack to cool.

MAKES 10

VARIATION
Substitute blueberries with fresh raspberries.

TIP
Be careful not to over-mix the batter as the blueberries can turn the mixture blue.

BACON-CHEDDAR MUFFINS

125 g (4½ oz) rindless bacon, chopped
250 g (8½ oz) plain flour
1 tbsp baking powder
scant ½ tsp salt
pinch of cayenne pepper
100 g (3½ oz) grated Cheddar cheese
1 tbsp chopped fresh parsley
2 large eggs
80 ml (2¾ fl oz) sunflower oil
250 ml (8½ fl oz) milk

1 Fry bacon, in a little oil if necessary, and set aside.

2 Sift flour, baking powder, salt and cayenne pepper. Add fried bacon, cheese and parsley.

3 In another bowl, whisk eggs, oil and milk together. Add to dry ingredients, mixing until just combined. Spoon into greased muffin cups, filling each to two-thirds full.

4 Bake in a preheated oven at 200 °C (400 °F, gas mark 6) for about 20 minutes, or until golden brown. Cool for a few minutes on a wire rack and serve warm with butter.

MAKES 12

TIP
Freeze the muffins in an airtight freezer bag for up to two months. Place in 750 watt microwave and defrost for about 2 minutes.

APRICOT, ORANGE AND BUTTERMILK MUFFINS

100 g (3½ oz) dried apricots, chopped
80 ml (2¾ fl oz) orange juice
250 g (8½ oz) self-raising flour
125 g (4½ oz) butter
105 g (3¾ oz) caster sugar
2 large eggs
200 ml (7 fl oz) buttermilk

1 Soak apricots in orange juice for about 30 minutes.

2 Sift flour and rub in butter until mixture resembles a coarse crumble.

3 In another bowl, whisk sugar, eggs and buttermilk and add, with apricot mix, to the flour mixture; the batter should still be lumpy.

4 Spoon mixture into greased muffin cups, filling each to two-thirds full.

5 Bake in a preheated oven at 180 °C (350 °F, gas mark 4) for 20–25 minutes, or until golden brown. Turn out onto a wire rack to cool.

MAKES 12

TIP
These muffins can be successfully frozen for up to three months.

Left to right: *Apricot, Orange and Buttermilk Muffins, Best-ever Blueberry Muffins, Bacon-Cheddar Muffins.*

SPICY CARROT MUFFINS

80 ml (2¾ fl oz) sunflower oil
100 g (3½ oz) caster sugar
2 large eggs
125 g (4½ oz) finely grated carrots
35 g (1¼ oz) seedless raisins
200 ml (7 fl oz) milk
scant ½ tsp vanilla essence
250 g (8½ oz) plain flour
1 tbsp baking powder
1 tsp bicarbonate of soda
1 tsp ground allspice
1 tsp ground cinnamon
scant ½ tsp salt
cinnamon-sugar for topping

1 Beat oil and sugar together. Add eggs and beat until mixture is light and fluffy. Add carrots, raisins, milk and vanilla essence.

2 Sift the flour, baking powder, bicarbonate of soda, allspice, cinnamon and salt together. Add wet mixture to flour mixture and mix until flour is moistened; batter should still be lumpy.

3 Spoon into greased muffin cups, filling each to two-thirds full. Sprinkle with cinnamon-sugar.

4 Bake in a preheated oven at 200 °C (400 °F, gas mark 6) for about 20 minutes, or until golden brown. Turn out onto a rack to cool.

MAKES 12

VARIATION
Substitute raisins with chopped nuts, such as walnuts or pecan nuts.

CITRUS MUFFINS

250 g (8½ oz) plain flour
scant ½ tsp bicarbonate of soda
1 tbsp baking powder
½ tsp salt
100 ml (3½ fl oz) sunflower oil
75 g (2½ oz) caster sugar
2 large eggs
125 ml (4 fl oz) plain yoghurt or buttermilk
125 ml (4 fl oz) grapefruit, orange or lemon juice
1 tsp grated grapefruit, orange or lemon rind

1 Sift flour, bicarbonate of soda, baking powder and salt together.

2 In another bowl, whisk oil and sugar together. Add eggs, yoghurt, juice and rind. Fold this mixture into flour mixture; batter should still be lumpy.

3 Spoon into greased muffin cups, filling each to two-thirds full. Bake in a preheated oven at 200 °C (400 °F, gas mark 6) for about 20 minutes. Turn out onto a wire rack to cool.

MAKES 12

VARIATION
Add 3 tbsp poppyseeds.

TIP
When grating orange or lemon rind, be careful to remove only the outside rind and not the white pith, which will result in a bitter taste.

HONEY-MUESLI MUFFINS

250 g (8½ oz) brown or wheatmeal flour
1 tbsp baking powder
scant ½ tsp salt
50 g (1¾ oz) soft brown sugar
70 g (2½ oz) muesli
1 large egg
200 ml (7 fl oz) milk
80 ml (2¾ fl oz) sunflower oil
65 g (2¼ oz) honey

1 Sift flour, baking powder and salt into a bowl. Add bran left behind in sieve. Add sugar and muesli.

2 In a separate bowl, whisk egg, milk, oil and honey.

3 Pour egg mixture into dry ingredients and mix until just combined. Do not over-mix; batter should still be lumpy.

4 Spoon into greased muffin cups, filling each to two-thirds full. Bake in a preheated oven at 200°C (400 °F, gas mark 6) for 15-20 minutes. Cool for a few minutes on a wire rack, then serve warm with butter.

MAKES 10

VARIATION
For a lighter texture, substitute the brown or wholewheat flour with 125 g (4½ oz) wholemeal flour and 125 g (4½ oz) plain white flour.

Clockwise from left: *Citrus Muffins, Honey-Muesli Muffins, Spicy Carrot Muffins.*

HEALTHY BRAN MUFFINS

2 large eggs
125 ml (4 fl oz) sunflower oil
300 g (10½ oz) soft brown sugar
500 ml (17 fl oz) milk
1 tsp vanilla essence
150 g (5½ oz) wholemeal flour
185 g (6½ oz) plain flour
1 tsp salt
2 tsp bicarbonate of soda
60 g (2 oz) wheat bran
150 g (5½ oz) mixed dried fruit
150 g (5½ oz) pitted dates,
chopped

1 Whisk eggs, oil, sugar and milk together. Add vanilla essence.

2 In a separate bowl, sift flours, salt and bicarbonate of soda. Add contents of sieve, then add wheat bran. Add dried fruit and dates.

3 Add wet mixture to dry ingredients and mix until combined. Spoon into well-greased muffin cups, filling each to two-thirds full. Bake in a preheated oven at 180 °C (350 °F, gas mark 4) for 20–25 minutes.

MAKES 24

VARIATION
Substitute the wheat bran with 150 g (5½ oz) additional wholemeal flour.

TIP
Store the mixture in an airtight container in the refrigerator for up to two weeks.

CAPPUCCINO MUFFINS

250 g (8½ oz) self-raising flour
scant ½ tsp bicarbonate of soda
scant ½ tsp salt
1 tbsp instant coffee powder
150 g (5½ oz) caster sugar
2 large eggs
125 ml (4 fl oz) milk
125 ml (4 fl oz) sunflower oil

1 Sift flour, bicarbonate of soda, salt and coffee powder together. Add sugar.

2 In another bowl, whisk eggs, milk and oil together. Fold this mixture into flour mixture; the batter should still be lumpy.

3 Spoon into greased muffin cups, filling each to two-thirds full. Bake in a preheated oven at 200 °C (400 °F, gas mark 6) for about 20 minutes, or until golden brown. Turn out onto a wire rack to cool.

MAKES 10

VARIATIONS
Add Tia Maria to egg mixture. To make double chocolate muffins: Omit coffee powder and add 50 g (1¾ oz) chocolate chips, 25 g (scant 1 oz) cocoa powder and 4 tbsp milk.

MANDARIN MUFFINS

185 g (6½ oz) plain flour
2 tsp baking powder
scant ½ tsp ground allspice
scant ½ tsp salt
100 g (3½ oz) caster sugar
1 large egg, beaten
200 ml (7 fl oz) milk
80 g (2¾ oz) butter, melted
310 g can mandarin orange
segments, drained

1 Sift together flour, baking powder, allspice and salt. Add sugar.

2 In another bowl, whisk egg, milk and melted butter. Add this mixture to dry ingredients, stirring until just combined. Add mandarins and stir in. Do not over-mix; the batter should still be lumpy.

3 Spoon into greased muffin cups, filling each to two-thirds full. Bake in a preheated oven at 200 °C (400 °F, gas mark 6) for 15–20 minutes, or until golden brown. Cool for a few minutes on a rack, then serve warm with butter.

MAKES 10

VARIATION
Substitute mandarins with any other drained, canned fruit of choice.

Left to right: *Healthy Bran Muffins, Mandarin Muffins.*

SCONES

Scone recipes usually contain an approximate liquid quantity as the moisture content of flour varies and the rate at which the flour absorbs the liquid will determine the amount required. Scone dough must be soft and sticky. When turning onto a lightly floured surface, dust your hands with flour. Don't use too much flour as this will result in dry scones and cause them to brown too much. Flatten the dough gently by hand to achieve an equal overall thickness, or use a rolling pin. Cut with a knife or a metal scone cutter.

The oven temperature should be very hot as scones need to rise quickly.

For a golden brown colour, brush with water, milk or beaten egg. If crusty scones are required, space them about 1 cm (½ in) apart. Alternatively, stack them close together on a greased baking tray and bake for slightly longer. This will result in upright scones with soft sides. To soften the crust, wrap hot scones in a tea towel.

CHEDDAR-DILL SCONES

280 g (10 oz) plain flour
1 tbsp baking powder
scant ½ tsp salt
125 g (4½ oz) butter or margarine
2 tbsp chopped fresh dill
or 2 tsp dried
50 g (1¾ oz) grated Cheddar cheese
1 large egg
about 100 ml (3½ fl oz) milk

1 Sift flour, baking powder and salt. Rub in butter and add dill and cheese.

2 In another bowl, beat egg and milk. Mix this into flour mixture until a soft dough is formed. Turn onto a lightly floured surface.

3 Divide dough in half. Roll each piece into a 20 cm (8 in) flattened ball. Cut each one into eight wedges.

4 Bake in a preheated oven at 200 °C (400 °F, gas mark 6) for 15–20 minutes until golden brown. Serve hot with butter.

MAKES 16 WEDGES

ORANGE-PUMPKIN SCONES

375 g (13 oz) plain flour
4 tsp baking powder
scant ½ tsp salt
2 tbsp caster sugar
4 tbsp milk
4 tbsp fresh orange juice
about 3 tbsp sunflower oil
1 large egg
1 tsp grated orange rind
250 g (8½ oz) cooked, mashed pumpkin

1 Sift flour, baking powder and salt. Add sugar.

2 In a separate bowl, whisk together milk, orange juice, oil, egg and rind. Mix this into dry ingredients. Add mashed pumpkin and lightly mix. Roll out to a thickness of 2 cm (¾ in). Stamp out with an 8 cm (7¼ in) scone cutter and bake in a preheated oven at 200 °C (400 °F, gas mark 6) for 10–12 minutes. Turn out onto a wire rack to cool.

MAKES 8

> ### VARIATION
> Substitute pumpkin with mashed butternut squash.

FRUIT SCONES

250 ml (8½ fl oz) hot, strong black tea
100 g (3½ oz) mixed dried fruit
250 g (8½ oz) self-raising flour
scant ½ tsp salt
½ tsp ground cinnamon
pinch of mixed spice
60 g (2 oz) butter or margarine
about 125 ml (4 fl oz) soured cream

1 Pour tea over fruit and leave for 20 minutes until mixture is cold.

2 Sift dry ingredients into a bowl and rub in butter. Stir in fruit with 100 ml (3½ fl oz) of the tea and enough soured cream and lightly mix to a soft dough.

3 Turn dough onto a floured surface. Press out to 2 cm (¾ in) thick and cut with a 6 cm (2½ in) scone cutter. Place on a greased baking tray. Bake in a preheated oven at 200 °C (400 °F, gas mark 6) for 12–15 minutes. Cool.

MAKES 10

> ### TIP
> Pack raw scones tightly together on a baking tray for a softer, more moist result.

Clockwise from left: *Fruit Scones, Cheddar-Dill Scones, Orange-Pumpkin Scones.*

BUTTERMILK SCONES

250 g (8½ oz) plain flour
1 tbsp baking powder
scant ½ tsp salt
2 tbsp caster sugar
125 g (4½ oz) butter
1 large egg
100 ml (3½ fl oz) buttermilk or
soured cream
3½ tbsp water

1 Sift flour, baking powder and salt together. Add sugar. Rub in butter until the mixture resembles fine breadcrumbs.

2 In a separate bowl, whisk egg, buttermilk and water.

3 Make a well in the centre of the flour mixture and pour in liquid. Mix to form a soft dough. Turn onto a lightly floured surface, pat lightly to 2 cm (¾ in) thick and cut into rounds with a 6 cm (2½ in) scone cutter.

4 Place scones on a greased baking tray. Bake in a preheated oven at 200 °C (400 °F, gas mark 6) for 12–15 minutes. Turn out onto a wire rack to cool.

MAKES ABOUT 10

VARIATIONS
Cheese scones: Add 100 g (3½ oz) grated Cheddar cheese to dough.
Herb scones: Add chopped fresh herbs to dry ingredients.
Date or nut scones: Add 75 g (2½ oz) chopped dates or nuts.

TIP
Buttermilk is an excellent baking ingredient. It can be substituted by adding 1 tbsp fresh lemon juice or vinegar to every 250 ml (8½ fl oz) milk. Leave the mixture to stand for about 5 minutes to thicken.

PIES AND SAVOURIES

Puff pastry is most successfully made with strong flour, with a little lemon juice added to soften the gluten and make the dough more elastic. Rolling and folding also form part of the method. Traditionally, shortcrust pastry is made with a mix of butter and lard, but today it is more often made with butter only for a richer flavour. If margarine is used, it should be the hard, block type.

PUFF PASTRY

280 g (10 oz) white bread flour
scant ½ tsp salt
250 g (8½ oz) cold butter
125 ml (4 fl oz) iced water
1 tsp fresh lemon juice

1 Sift flour and salt. Press butter into a 15 cm (6 in) flat square and keep chilled.

2 Mix water with lemon juice, pour over flour and cut in with a knife. Mix until smooth, forming a stiff dough.

3 Roll out pastry on a lightly floured surface to a thickness of 5 mm (¼ in), keeping it rectangular.

4 Place butter in centre of dough and fold corners to the middle to make an envelope, enclosing butter.

5 Roll out pastry again. Fold in three by turning bottom third up and top third over the previous fold. Seal edges, then roll and fold in three again. Chill for 30 minutes.

6 Repeat rolling and folding pastry seven times, chilling when necessary.

7 Roll out and refrigerate for at least 30 minutes before using, or freeze for up to three months.

MAKES ABOUT 600 G (1 LB 5 OZ) PASTRY

CREAMY BACON PLAIT

40 g (1¼ oz) butter or margarine
2 tbsp plain flour
250 ml (8½ fl oz) milk
1 tbsp sunflower oil
125 g (4½ oz) rindless streaky
bacon, chopped
1 medium onion, chopped
1 medium green pepper,
seeded and chopped
125 g (4½ oz) button mushrooms,
sliced (optional)
2 tsp chopped fresh mixed herbs
or ½ tsp dried
salt and freshly ground black
pepper to taste
300 g (10½ oz) puff pastry (see left)
beaten egg or milk to glaze
2 tbsp sesame seeds for topping

1 Melt butter in a saucepan. Add flour, stirring over low heat for 1 minute. Add milk, stirring constantly until smooth and thick. Set aside.

2 Heat oil in a saucepan and fry bacon until crisp. Add onion, green pepper and mushrooms and sauté until just soft. Add herbs, salt and pepper and leave to cool slightly.

3 Roll out pastry to a thickness of 3 mm (⅛ in) and shape into a rectangle.

4 Mix white sauce and bacon mixture. Spoon into centre of pastry, leaving both sides open.

5 Cut sides diagonally into 1–1.5 cm (about ⅝ in) strips and plait by folding over filling. Place on a greased baking tray. Brush with beaten egg or milk and sprinkle with sesame seeds. Bake in a preheated oven at 200 °C (400 °F, gas mark 6) for 30–35 minutes.

SERVES 4–6

CHIVE-ONION TWISTS

15 g (½ oz) butter
1 medium onion, finely chopped
4 tbsp chopped fresh chives
300 g (10½ oz) puff pastry
(see far left)
1 tbsp milk
50 g (1¾ oz) grated Cheddar cheese

1 Melt butter in a saucepan. Sauté onion and chives until soft. Set aside.

2 Roll pastry into a 3 mm (⅛ in) thick rectangle. Spread onion mixture over one half. Cover with remaining pastry. Brush with milk and sprinkle with cheese. Roll lightly.

3 Cut pastry into 2 cm (¾ in) wide strips of about 8 cm (7¼ in) in length. Twist strips and place on greased baking trays. Brush lightly with milk. Bake in a preheated oven at 200 °C (400 °F, gas mark 6) for 12–15 minutes.

MAKES 14

Creamy Bacon Plait

VENISON AND BACON PIE

300 g (10½ oz) puff pastry
(see page 80)
1 large egg, beaten

MARINADE
125 ml (4 fl oz) dry red wine
100 ml (3½ fl oz) buttermilk
1 tbsp Worcestershire sauce
(optional)

FILLING
1.5 kg (3 lb 3 oz) venison, cubed
3½ tbsp sunflower oil
2 large onions, coarsely chopped
250 g (8½ oz) rindless streaky
bacon, chopped
3–4 cloves garlic, crushed
about 750 ml (1¼ pints) meat stock
100 ml (3½ fl oz) red wine
1 tbsp chopped fresh thyme
or 1 tsp dried
salt and freshly ground black
pepper to taste
5 carrots, quartered, or
300 g (10½ oz) baby carrots

1 For marinade: mix all ingredients well. Marinate venison overnight, or for at least 6 hours.

2 For filling: heat oil in a large, heavy-based saucepan and sauté onions, bacon and garlic until soft. Remove venison from marinade with a slotted spoon. Add to onion mixture and brown.

3 Add stock, wine, thyme and seasoning. Bring to the boil, reduce heat and simmer for 2½–3 hours. Add more stock if necessary.

4 Add carrots and simmer for a further 20 minutes. Thicken slightly with flour if necessary. Spoon into a large ovenproof dish. Roll out pastry to a thickness of 3 mm (⅛ in) and cover dish. Crimp edges and brush with egg. Bake in a preheated oven at 220 °C (425 °F, gas mark 7) for 15–20 minutes, or until pastry is golden brown.

SERVES 4–6

VARIATION
Make mini pies in deep bun tins and bake for about 20 minutes.

TIP
The flavour of garlic, like that of onion, softens if you simmer it in liquid.

FRUITY PORK PIE

2 tbsp sunflower oil
500 g (1 lb 2 oz) pork sausages
1 large onion, chopped
2 medium potatoes, cut into cubes
75 g (2½ oz) seedless raisins
1 tbsp chopped fresh oregano
or 1 tsp dried
scant ½ tsp ground cinnamon
250 ml (8½ fl oz) beef stock
2 tart apples, peeled,
cored and sliced
125 ml (4 fl oz) apple juice
1 tbsp plain flour
salt and freshly ground black
pepper to taste
300 g (10½ oz) puff pastry
(see page 80)
beaten egg or milk to glaze

1 Heat oil in a heavy-based saucepan. Brown sausages; remove and cut into slices.

2 Return sausages to saucepan. Stir in onion, potatoes, raisins, oregano and cinnamon and cook for a few minutes over medium heat.

3 Add stock, apples and apple juice. Cover and simmer for 10–15 minutes.

4 Mix flour with 2 tbsp water, add to mixture and boil until it thickens. Add seasoning and leave to cool.

5 Roll half the pastry to a thickness of 3 mm (⅛ in) and line a large greased pie plate. Fill with cooked mixture.

6 Roll out remainder of dough to a thickness of 3 mm (⅛ in) and cover pie. Seal edges with water and slash pastry lid with a knife or lattice pastry cutter. Brush with beaten egg or milk.

7 Bake in a preheated oven at 200 °C (400 °F, gas mark 6) for 30–40 minutes.

SERVES 6

VARIATION
Make individual pies.

TIP
If pastry takes too long to brown and the filling boils out, add a little dried milk and caster sugar to the dough recipe the next time you make it. The pastry will taste better and will brown quickly.

Left to right: *Fruity Pork Pies, Venison and Bacon Pie.*

CRUSTLESS ASPARAGUS FLAN

100 g (3½ oz) butter
1 onion, chopped
85 g (3 oz) plain flour
290 g can asparagus pieces
500 ml (17 fl oz) milk
125 g (4½ oz) feta cheese, crumbled
125 g (4½ oz) button mushrooms, sliced
2 tbsp chopped fresh parsley or 2 tsp dried
1 tsp prepared mustard
scant ½ tsp salt
pinch of cayenne pepper
3 large eggs, beaten

1 Heat 20 g (¾ oz) butter in a heavy-based saucepan. Add onion and sauté until soft. Remove and set aside.

2 Melt remaining butter and stir in flour. Drain asparagus liquid from can and add with milk to butter mixture. Boil until it thickens.

3 Remove from heat and add fried onion, asparagus and all remaining ingredients. Stir gently to prevent asparagus breaking up.

4 Spoon into a 24 cm (9½ in) square ovenproof dish. Bake in a preheated oven at 180 °C (350 °F, gas mark 4) for 30–40 minutes until golden.

SERVES 4–6

TIP
To preserve herbs, hang them in a dry, dark place. This concentrates the essential oils and provides a store of flavour for cooking.

CHICKEN AND PASTA PIE

125 g (4½ oz) pasta shells
4 chicken breasts, skinned and boned (about 500 g/1 lb 2 oz)
1 tbsp sunflower oil
125 g (4½ oz) rindless streaky bacon, chopped
2 medium onions, chopped
salt and freshly ground black pepper to taste
30 g (1 oz) butter or margarine
40 g (1¼ oz) plain flour
600 ml (1 pint) milk

TOPPING
60 g (2 oz) grated mozzarella cheese
1 tbsp dried breadcrumbs

1 Cook pasta, drain and set aside. Simmer chicken in a little stock or water until cooked, then drain and cut into small pieces.

2 Heat oil in heavy-based saucepan and sauté bacon and onions until soft. Add chicken, pasta and seasoning, mix and spoon into a 24 cm (9½ in) square ovenproof dish.

3 Heat butter in a heavy-based saucepan. Add flour and stir over heat for a minute. Add milk and stir while boiling until it thickens. Pour over chicken mixture.

4 For topping: sprinkle cheese and crumbs over the top of the pie and bake in a preheated oven at 180 °C (350 °F, gas mark 4) for 15–20 minutes.

SERVES 4–6

SAVOURY FRITTERS

185 g (6½ oz) self-raising flour
½ tsp salt
250 ml (8½ fl oz) milk
2 large eggs
100 g (3½ oz) grated Cheddar cheese
125 g (4½ oz) rindless streaky bacon, chopped and fried
1 tbsp chopped fresh parsley or 1 tsp dried
oil for frying

1 Sift flour and salt together. In another bowl, whisk milk and eggs and beat gradually into flour mixture.

2 Add cheese, bacon and parsley and mix lightly.

3 Shallow-fry tablespoonfuls of mixture in hot oil until brown on both sides. Serve hot.

MAKES ABOUT 15

VARIATION
Substitute cheese and bacon with 170 g can tuna, drained, or 420 g can cream-style sweetcorn.

TIP
Fry the fritters in hot oil. If the oil is too cold, too much of the oil will be soaked up and will result in soggy fritters.

Clockwise from top: *Crustless Asparagus Flan, Chicken and Pasta Pie, Savoury Fritters.*

CRUMBED CHICKEN STRIPS

500 g (1 lb 2 oz) skinned and
boned chicken breasts,
cut into strips
125 g (4½ oz) plain flour
2 large eggs, beaten
240 g (8¼ oz) dried breadcrumbs
50 g (1¾ oz) butter or margarine
125 ml (4 fl oz) olive oil
2 cloves garlic, crushed

1 Coat strips of chicken in flour.
Dip into beaten egg, then into
breadcrumbs. Refrigerate for at
least 30 minutes for crumbs to set.

2 Heat butter and olive oil in a heavy-
based pan. Add crushed garlic and fry
chicken in batches until golden-brown.

3 Remove each batch and drain
on kitchen paper. Serve with freshly
squeezed lemon juice or any sauce
of choice.

SERVES 4–6

VARIATIONS
Substitute the chicken with
steak or fish.
The crumbed chicken can also
be deep-fried.

TIP
To make dried breadcrumbs, bake
slices of bread in an oven until
crisp, then crush with a rolling pin.
Store in an airtight container for
up to one month.

POTATO BAKE

2 large potatoes
250 ml (8½ fl oz) soured cream
50 g (1¾ oz) grated Cheddar cheese
415 g can cream of chicken soup
2 tbsp chopped spring onions
salt and freshly ground black
pepper to taste
60 g (2 oz) dried breadcrumbs
40 g (1¼ oz) wholemeal flour
30 g (1 oz) butter or margarine,
melted
1 tbsp chopped fresh parsley
or 1 tsp dried

1 Peel and slice the potatoes and
parboil slightly. Layer them in a large
ovenproof dish.

2 Mix soured cream, cheese, soup,
onions and seasoning and pour over
the potatoes.

3 Mix crumbs, flour and butter and
sprinkle over potatoes. Top with parsley.

4 Bake in a preheated oven at 180 °C
(350 °F, gas mark 4) for 40 minutes.

SERVES 4

VARIATIONS
Substitute Cheddar cheese with
any other cheese of choice.
Substitute cream of chicken soup
with any other flavour.

CHEESE AND CHILLI PUFFS

125 g (4½ oz) self-raising flour
1 tsp baking powder
pinch of salt
scant ½ tsp mustard powder
1½ tsp crushed dried chillies
100 g (3½ oz) grated Cheddar cheese
1 large egg
125 ml (4 fl oz) milk
15 g (½ oz) butter or margarine,
melted

1 Sift flour, baking powder, salt
and mustard powder together. Add
crushed chillies and cheese.

2 In another bowl, whisk egg, milk
and melted butter.

3 Add to dry ingredients and mix
until just combined.

4 Spoon into greased deep bun
tins and bake in a preheated oven
at 200 °C (400 °F, gas mark 6) for
10–12 minutes. Serve warm.

MAKES ABOUT 12 SMALL OR 6 LARGE

VARIATIONS
Substitute dried chillies with
scant ½ tsp cayenne pepper.
Add a few pieces of chopped
ham or bacon if liked.

Clockwise from top left: *Cheese and Chilli Puffs, Crumbed Chicken Strips, Camembert Fritters.*

CAMEMBERT FRITTERS

30 g (1 oz) plain flour
scant ½ tsp paprika
125 g (4½ oz) camembert, cut into
8 wedges
2 large eggs, beaten
60 g (2 oz) dried breadcrumbs
oil for deep-frying

1 Sift flour and paprika. Dip cheese wedges into flour mix.

2 Dip into egg then breadcrumbs. Press well to coat completely.

3 Refrigerate for 30 minutes to set and prevent crumbs from falling off.

4 Deep-fry in hot oil for about 2 minutes until golden brown. Drain on kitchen paper and serve immediately as a starter.

SERVES 4

TIP
To make flavoured oils: Place chosen herbs in bottle or jar, top with oil and leave to infuse for 3–4 weeks. Olive oil with bay leaves and rosemary makes a good basting for barbecues.

ONION RINGS IN BATTER

2 large onions, cut into thick rings
extra flour for coating
oil for deep-frying

BATTER
155 g (5½ oz) self-raising flour
½ tsp salt
1 tsp paprika
1 tbsp poppy seeds or sesame seeds
250 ml (8½ fl oz) water or beer

1 Sift flour, salt and paprika. Add seeds and water. Mix well and leave to stand for at least 30 minutes.

2 Dip onion rings into extra flour, then into batter and deep fry in hot oil until golden. Serve with tartare sauce or sweet-and-sour sauce.

SERVES 4–6

TANDOORI CHICKEN WRAPS

FILLING
4 chicken breasts, skinned and boned (about 600 g/1 lb 5 oz)
3 tbsp fresh lemon juice

MARINADE
1 onion, chopped
3 cloves garlic, crushed
2 tbsp chopped fresh root ginger
½ tsp turmeric
1 green chilli, seeded and chopped
2 tsp curry powder
scant ½ tsp ground cumin
175 ml (6 fl oz) plain yoghurt

DOUGH
375 g (13 oz) plain flour
2 tsp baking powder
scant ½ tsp salt
2 tbsp olive or sunflower oil
1 tsp white vinegar
about 200 ml (7 fl oz) lukewarm water
45 g (1½ oz) butter
extra butter for frying

1 For filling: cut chicken into large cubes. Sprinkle with lemon juice and set aside for about 10 minutes.

2 For marinade: mix together all ingredients and pour over chicken pieces. Cover and leave to marinate for 4–6 hours, or overnight if possible.

3 For dough: sift flour, baking powder and salt together.

4 Mix oil, vinegar and water and mix into dry ingredients. Knead dough until soft and elastic. Roll out on a floured surface until about 5 mm (¼ in) thick.

5 Spread with butter and roll up tightly like a Swiss roll. Cut into 5 cm (2 in) thick slices (about 12 slices). Flatten each slice slightly by hand and roll out into 23 cm (9 in) rounds. Leave to rest for 20–30 minutes.

6 Heat pan and fry dough rounds in butter for 1 minute per side. Remove chicken from marinade and fry until cooked. Fill fried pastries and roll up.

MAKES 12–14

VARIATION
Fill with roasted vegetables.

FISH PIE

POTATO CASE
125 g (4½ oz) plain flour
1½ tsp baking powder
scant ½ tsp salt
60 g (2 oz) butter or margarine, melted
250 g (8½ oz) mashed potato

FILLING
15 g (½ oz) butter
1 onion, chopped
2 tbsp plain flour
250 ml (8½ fl oz) milk
2 large eggs
2 hard-boiled eggs, chopped
2 x 170 g cans tuna chunks in water, drained
1 tbsp chopped fresh parsley or 1 tsp dried
1 tbsp chopped fresh mixed herbs or 1 tsp dried
salt and freshly ground black pepper to taste
pinch of cayenne pepper

1 For case: sift dry ingredients. Add butter and mashed potato. Mix well. Press into base and sides of a greased 24 cm (9½ in) square ovenproof dish.

2 For filling: heat butter in a heavy-based pan and sauté onion until soft. Mix in all other ingredients and spoon into potato case. Bake in a preheated oven at 180 °C (350 °F, gas mark 4) for 35–40 minutes.

SERVES 4–6

TIP
To avoid tears when chopping onions, chill them before chopping.

Clockwise from top: *Fish Pie, Onion Rings in Batter, Tandoori Chicken Wraps.*

MINCE PIE WITH COBBLER TOPPING

FILLING

500 g (1 lb 2 oz) lean beef mince
125 g (4½ oz) rindless streaky
bacon, chopped
2 onions, chopped
2 sticks celery, chopped
1 green pepper, seeded
and chopped
50 g (1¾ oz) tomato paste
2 tsp caster sugar
250 ml (8½ fl oz) meat stock
4 tbsp dry red wine (optional)
salt and freshly ground black
pepper to taste

TOPPING

185 g (6½ oz) self-raising flour
1 tsp salt
4 tbsp wheat bran
2 tbsp chopped fresh chives
or 2 tsp dried
1 tbsp chopped fresh parsley
or 1 tsp dried
50 g (1¾ oz) grated Cheddar cheese
125 ml (4 fl oz) milk

1 For filling: fry mince until colour
changes. Add bacon and fry until
starting to brown. Add onions, celery
and green pepper and sauté until soft.

2 Add tomato paste, sugar, stock,
wine and seasoning and simmer for
about 10 minutes.

3 For topping: sift the flour and salt
and add the bran. Add the chives,
parsley and cheese.

4 Add milk and mix lightly into a
soft dough. Roll out on a lightly
floured surface to a thickness of about
1–1.5 cm (about ⅝ in). Stamp out
rounds with a 6 cm (2½ in) cutter.

5 Spoon mince into a large ovenproof dish and top with scone rounds.
Bake in a preheated oven at 180 °C
(350 °F, gas mark 4) for 30–40 minutes.

SERVES 4–6

> ### TIP
> When flouring a surface to knead
> on or roll out pastry, use a flour
> shaker to prevent too much flour
> being absorbed by the pastry.

COURGETTE FRITTERS

125 g (4½ oz) grated courgettes
2 large eggs, beaten
1 onion, chopped
30 g (1 oz) plain flour
60 g (2 oz) grated mozzarella
cheese
salt and freshly ground black
pepper to taste
oil for frying

1 Mix together courgettes, eggs,
onion, flour, cheese and seasoning.

2 Heat the oil in a large saucepan.
Drop tablespoonfuls of mixture into
the oil and cook for a few minutes on
each side, until golden brown. Drain
on kitchen paper and serve hot.

MAKES ABOUT 12

MINCE VETKOEKIES

250 g (8½ oz) self-raising flour
1 tsp baking powder
1 tsp salt
2 tsp chopped fresh parsley
or ½ tsp dried
2 large eggs
250 ml (8½ fl oz) water
1 tbsp sunflower oil
200 g (7 oz) lean beef mince
sunflower oil for deep-frying

1 Sift flour, baking powder and
salt. Add parsley. Beat eggs and
water, add to dry ingredients and
mix well.

2 Heat oil in heavy-based saucepan
and fry mince until the colour
changes. Add the mince to flour
mixture and mix well.

3 Spoon tablespoonfuls into hot oil
and deep-fry until light brown.

MAKES ABOUT 30

> ### TIP
> Parsley is the best known and
> most used of all herbs. It enhances
> the flavour of sauces, soups, stews
> and stuffings, and is used as part
> of a classic bouquet garni.

Top to bottom: *Mince Pie with Cobbler Topping, Courgette Fritters, Mince Vetkoekies.*

RATATOUILLE CRÊPES

CRÊPES
125 g (4½ oz) plain flour
scant ½ tsp salt
2 large eggs
150 ml (5 fl oz) water
about 200 ml (7 fl oz) milk

RATATOUILLE FILLING
1 tbsp olive oil
1 onion, sliced
1 clove garlic, crushed
1 medium green pepper, seeded
and chopped
4 courgettes, chopped
1 tbsp chopped fresh oregano
or 1 tsp dried
2 medium ripe tomatoes, chopped
2 tbsp tomato paste
salt and freshly ground black
pepper to taste
2 tbsp freshly grated
Parmesan cheese

1 For crêpes: sift flour and salt. Whisk eggs with water and add to flour with enough milk to make a thin batter. Set aside for at least 1 hour.

2 Lightly oil a heavy-based frying pan and heat. For each crêpe, pour in just enough batter to cover base of pan and fry until lightly browned on both sides.

3 For filling: heat oil, add onion and garlic and sauté until soft. Add green pepper, courgettes, oregano, tomatoes, paste and seasoning. Heat until soft.

4 Spoon the filling onto the crêpes, sprinkle with cheese and fold into quarters or roll up.

MAKES 15, DEPENDING ON SIZE OF PAN

LEEK FLANS

CREAM CHEESE PASTRY
125 g (4½ oz) plain flour
scant ½ tsp salt
100 g (3½ oz) butter
100 g (3½ oz) cream cheese
1 tsp poppy or sesame seeds

FILLING
30 g (1 oz) butter
2 medium leeks, thinly sliced
125 g (4½ oz) button mushrooms,
sliced
30 g (1 oz) freshly grated Parmesan
cheese
250 ml (8½ fl oz) milk
3 large eggs, lightly beaten
1 tbsp chopped fresh mixed herbs
or 1 tsp dried
salt and freshly ground black
pepper to taste

1 For pastry: sift flour and salt. Rub in butter until mixture resembles breadcrumbs. Mix in cream cheese and seeds. Turn onto a floured board, knead until smooth, cover and refrigerate for 30 minutes. Press into tartlet tins.

2 Line flan cases with greaseproof paper, fill with dried beans and bake in a preheated oven at 200 °C (400 °F, gas mark 6) for about 7 minutes. Remove beans and paper.

3 For filling: melt butter, add leeks and mushrooms and fry until soft. Spoon mixture into flan cases and sprinkle with cheese. Mix milk, eggs, herbs and seasoning and pour over cheese. Bake in a preheated oven at 180 °C (350 °F, gas mark 4) for 20–25 minutes.

MAKES 6 SMALL OR 1 LARGE

BOBOTIE PIE

SWEET POTATO CASE
125 g (4½ oz) self-raising flour
½ tsp salt
60 g (2 oz) butter or margarine
250 g (8½ oz) cooked, mashed
sweet potatoes
1 large egg yolk, beaten

FILLING
2 tbsp sunflower oil
500 g (1 lb 2 oz) lean beef mince
1 onion, chopped
2 cloves garlic, crushed
½ tsp ground ginger
1 tbsp fruit chutney
2 tsp mild curry powder
1 tbsp chopped fresh mixed herbs
or 1 tsp dried
pinch of turmeric
50 g (1¾ oz) dried apricots
375 ml (12½ fl oz) milk
2 large eggs, lightly beaten
salt and freshly ground black
pepper to taste

1 For case: sift flour and salt. Rub in butter and add sweet potatoes. Mix with egg yolk and press onto the greased bottom and sides of a 24 cm (9½ in) ovenproof dish. Bake in a preheated oven at 180 °C (350 °F, gas mark 4) for 10 minutes.

2 For filling: heat oil in a heavy-based saucepan and fry mince until colour changes. Add onion and garlic and sauté until soft.

3 Add remaining ingredients, mix well and spoon into case. Bake for 35–40 minutes until set.

SERVES 4–6

Clockwise from top: *Leek Flans, Bobotie Pie, Ratatouille Crêpes.*

VEGETABLE QUICHE

CHEESE PASTRY
60 g (2 oz) plain flour
75 g (2½ oz) wholemeal flour
100 g (3½ oz) grated Cheddar
cheese
125 g (4½ oz) butter
1 tsp poppy seeds

FILLING
3 courgettes, sliced
200 g (7 oz) broccoli florets
30 g (1 oz) butter
1 clove garlic, crushed
25 g (scant 1 oz) sun-dried
tomatoes, chopped
1 onion, chopped
2 tsp caster sugar
125 g (4½ oz) sieved cottage cheese
200 ml (7 fl oz) milk or cream
2 large eggs
2 tbsp chopped fresh mixed herbs
or 2 tsp dried
salt and freshly ground black
pepper to taste
Parmesan cheese for topping

1 For pastry: mix all ingredients in a food processor until combined. Press the mixture into a greased 23 cm (9 in) flan dish.

2 For filling: blanch courgettes and broccoli for 1–2 minutes. Drain.

3 Heat butter in a heavy-based saucepan and sauté garlic, sun-dried tomatoes and onion until soft. Add sugar. Spoon the vegetables into the pastry case.

4 Beat cottage cheese, milk, eggs, herbs and seasoning together and pour over vegetables.

5 Sprinkle with Parmesan cheese and bake in a preheated oven at 160 °C (325 °F, gas mark 3) for 30–40 minutes.

SERVES 4–6

VARIATION
Substitute sun-dried tomatoes with 50 g (1¾ oz) cherry tomatoes.

TIP
A food processor is ideal for making this pastry. You can prepare pastry ahead and store it in the freezer for a few months.

MINCE PIZZA

BASE
280 g (10 oz) white bread flour
scant ½ tsp salt
½ tsp caster sugar
2 tsp easy-blend yeast
2 tbsp olive oil
about 125 ml (4 fl oz)
lukewarm water

MINCE TOPPING
410 g can tomato passata
2 cloves garlic, crushed
1 green pepper, seeded and sliced
500 g (1 lb 2 oz) lean beef mince
3 tbsp tomato paste
2 tsp caster sugar
4 tbsp dry white wine
4 tbsp meat stock
1 tbsp chopped fresh mixed herbs
or 1 tsp dried
salt and freshly ground black
pepper to taste
2 tbsp freshly grated Parmesan
cheese

1 For base: sift flour and salt. Add sugar and yeast and mix.

2 Add oil and water to mix to a soft dough. Knead until dough is smooth and elastic.

3 Cover with oiled cling film and leave in a warm place until doubled in size.

4 Knock back and divide in two. Flatten and spread out each piece on a greased 25 cm (10 in) pizza tin.

5 For topping: heat tomato passata, add garlic and green pepper and simmer for a few minutes. Spread onto base. Fry mince with all other ingredients, except cheese. Spread on top of pizza. Sprinkle with grated cheese and leave to prove for about 20 minutes.

6 Bake in a preheated oven at 200 °C (400 °F, gas mark 6) for 20 minutes.

MAKES 2 LARGE PIZZAS

VARIATION
Add or substitute other ingredients of your choice.

TIP
Pizzas on a yeast dough base, baked or unbaked, can be frozen successfully for up to one month, provided topping ingredients are suitable for freezing. Bake frozen, cooked pizza in a preheated oven at 200 °C (400 °F, gas mark 6) for 15 minutes, and frozen, uncooked pizza for about 30 minutes.

Clockwise from top left: *Mince Pizza, Spinach Pie, Vegetable Quiche.*

SPINACH PIE

SHORTCRUST PASTRY
250 g (8½ oz) plain flour
scant ½ tsp salt
125 g (4½ oz) cold butter
125 ml (4 fl oz) iced water
1 tsp fresh lemon juice or brandy

FILLING
60 g pkt dry onion soup mix
250 ml (8½ fl oz) soured cream
500 g (1 lb 2 oz) fresh spinach
30 g (1 oz) butter or margarine
125 g (4½ oz) button mushrooms,
sliced
250 g (8½ oz) sieved cottage cheese
3 large eggs, beaten
salt and black pepper to taste
scant ½ tsp mustard powder
50 g (1¾ oz) grated Cheddar cheese

1 For pastry: sift flour and salt together. Cut butter into small pieces and rub into flour until mixture resembles breadcrumbs.

2 Mix water and lemon juice into mixture to make a stiff dough. Cover with cling film and refrigerate for 30 minutes.

3 Roll out dough on a lightly floured surface to a thickness of 3 mm (⅛ in). Use to line the bottom and sides of a 24 cm (9½ in) ovenproof dish.

4 For filling: mix soup powder and soured cream.

5 Wash spinach, blanch until soft, drain well and chop finely.

6 Heat butter and sauté mushrooms. Mix together mushrooms, spinach and soured cream mixture.

7 Add the remaining ingredients and mix well.

8 Spoon filling into pie case. Bake in a preheated oven at 200 °C (400 °F, gas mark 6) for 35–40 minutes.

SERVES 4–6

TIP
To prevent the smell given off by cabbage, spinach and cauliflower when cooking, add a couple of bay leaves to the water.

DESSERTS

Everyone loves dessert, from light fruit, crêpes and crumbles, to heavier puddings, pies, baked puddings and cheesecakes. Most of these recipes can be made the day before and refrigerated until serving time. This will allow simple and quick heating and will release you from spending unnecessary time in the kitchen.

GOLDEN DUMPLINGS

SAUCE
375 ml (12½ fl oz) water
200 g (7 oz) granulated sugar
2 tbsp golden syrup
30 g (1 oz) butter or margarine
½ tsp mixed spice

DOUGH
125 g (4½ oz) self-raising flour
scant ½ tsp salt
scant ½ tsp bicarbonate of soda
30 g (1 oz) butter or margarine
1 tsp caster sugar
1 large egg
4 tbsp milk

1 For sauce: combine all ingredients in a saucepan and stir over moderate heat until the sugar has dissolved.

2 For dough: sift flour, salt and bicarbonate of soda. Rub in butter until crumbly. Add sugar and mix.

3 Whisk egg and milk together and add to dry ingredients. Mix until a soft dough is formed.

4 Bring sauce to the boil and spoon teaspoonfuls of dough into it. Reduce heat, cover and simmer for about 12–15 minutes without removing lid. Serve hot.

SERVES 4–6

FRUITY PUDDING

250 g (8½ oz) self-raising flour
½ tsp salt
2 tsp bicarbonate of soda
300 g (10½ oz) caster sugar
2 large eggs
520 g can fruit cocktail,
including syrup

SAUCE
200 g (7 oz) granulated sugar
170 g can evaporated milk
1 tsp vanilla essence
50 g (1¾ oz) butter or margarine

1 Sift flour, salt and bicarbonate of soda. Add sugar, eggs and fruit cocktail, including syrup. Mix well.

2 Pour the mixture into a large, greased ovenproof dish and bake in a preheated oven at 160 °C (325 °F, gas mark 3) for about 45 minutes.

3 For sauce: place all ingredients in a saucepan. Heat gently and stir until the sugar has dissolved. Boil for 1 minute.

4 Remove pudding from the oven when baked and pour the sauce over the hot pudding.

SERVES 4–6

SPICY APPLE CRUMBLE

FILLING
385 g can apple pie filling
2 tbsp fresh lemon juice
1½ tsp ground cinnamon
or mixed spice
40 g (1¼ oz) seedless raisins

TOPPING
60 g (2 oz) brown or
wheatmeal flour
100 g (3½ oz) soft brown sugar
40 g (1¼ oz) rolled oats
80 g (2¾ oz) butter or margarine

1 For filling: place apples in a 23 cm (9 in) greased pie dish. Sprinkle with lemon juice and cinnamon. Top with raisins.

2 For topping: sift flour. Add bran left over in sieve, and sugar and oats. Rub in butter. The crumble should be fairly coarse.

3 Sprinkle crumble over apples and bake in a preheated oven at 180 °C (350 °F, gas mark 4) for about 20 minutes, or until topping turns light brown and crisp.

SERVES 4–6

Crêpes with Creamy Banana and Caramel (page 102)

APRICOT STEAMED PUDDING

165 g (5¾ oz) apricot jam
125 g (4½ oz) butter or margarine
105 g (3¾ oz) caster sugar
2 large eggs, beaten
½ tsp vanilla essence
155 g (5½ oz) self-raising flour
scant ½ tsp salt
4 tbsp milk

1 Grease a 2 litre (3½ pint) pudding basin. Spoon the jam into the bottom and set aside.

2 Cream the butter and sugar. Add eggs, one at a time, beating well after each addition, until light and fluffy. Add vanilla essence.

3 Sift flour and salt and fold in. Add milk and mix well. Spoon mixture into the basin and level it with a spoon. Cover the pudding with a double layer of foil or greaseproof paper and secure with string or a lid.

4 Half-fill a heavy-based saucepan with boiling water. Place the pudding basin in the pan, cover and simmer for 1½–2 hours, checking the water regularly to make sure the pan doesn't boil dry. Uncover the pudding and turn out onto a serving plate. Serve hot.

SERVES 4–6

TIP
It is easy to forget to check the water level in the steamer. Put 2–3 small pebbles in the bottom of the pan; when they rattle loudly, the water level has dropped too low.

PINEAPPLE AND COCONUT PUDDING

SAUCE
2 tbsp plain flour
200 ml (7 fl oz) boiling water
200 g (7 oz) granulated sugar
scant ½ tsp salt
60 g (2 oz) butter or margarine
1 tsp lemon essence

SPONGE
1 large egg
100 g (3½ oz) caster sugar
185 g (6½ oz) plain flour
2 tsp baking powder
scant ½ tsp salt
125 ml (4 fl oz) milk
100 g (3½ oz) butter or margarine, melted
440 g can crushed pineapple
40 g (1¼ oz) desiccated coconut

1 For sauce: mix together flour, water, sugar, salt and butter and boil for about 3 minutes. Remove from heat and add lemon essence. Pour into a large ovenproof dish.

2 For sponge: beat egg and sugar together. Sift flour, baking powder and salt and fold in, alternating with milk and melted butter. Mix until smooth. Add pineapple and coconut and mix.

3 Pour sponge mixture over sauce and bake in a preheated oven at 180 °C (350 °F, gas mark 4) for about 45 minutes. Serve hot with cream or custard.

SERVES 4–6

GINGER PUDDING

200 g (7 oz) butter or margarine
1 large egg
250 ml (8½ fl oz) milk
200 g (7 oz) caster sugar
250 g (8½ oz) plain flour
2 tsp bicarbonate of soda
1 tbsp ground ginger
2 tbsp smooth apricot jam
4 tbsp chopped glacé ginger (optional)

SYRUP
125 g (4½ oz) granulated sugar
160 ml (5½ fl oz) water
1 tsp vanilla essence
45 g (1½ oz) butter

1 Melt butter, remove from heat and add egg, milk and caster sugar. Whisk well together.

2 Sift flour, bicarbonate of soda and ginger. Add to butter mixture, with apricot jam and glacé ginger. Mix well and pour into a large, deep ovenproof dish.

3 Bake in a preheated oven at 180 °C (350 °F, gas mark 4) for 20 minutes. Reduce temperature to 160 °C (325 °F, gas mark 3) and bake for another 20–25 minutes.

4 For syrup: melt all ingredients together and pour over pudding as soon as it is taken out of the oven.

SERVES 4–6

Clockwise from top: *Apricot Steamed Pudding, Pineapple and Coconut Pudding, Ginger Pudding.*

STICKY DATE PUDDING

100 g (3½ oz) dried dates, chopped
250 ml (8½ fl oz) water
155 g (5½ oz) plain flour
100 g (3½ oz) caster sugar
1½ tsp baking powder
1 tsp bicarbonate of soda
scant ½ tsp salt
4 tbsp sunflower oil or melted butter
4 tbsp milk
1 large egg

SAUCE
125 ml (4 fl oz) milk
50 g (1¾ oz) light brown sugar
60 g (2 oz) butter or margarine

1 Put dates and water into a pan and bring to the boil. Remove from heat. Leave to stand for 5 minutes to cool.

2 Sift all dry ingredients together. In another bowl, whisk oil, milk and egg and add, with date mixture, to dry ingredients. Mix well.

3 Spoon into a large, greased ovenproof dish. Bake in a preheated oven at 180 °C (350 °F, gas mark 4) for 40–45 minutes.

4 For sauce: mix all ingredients together and boil for 5 minutes. Pour sauce over hot pudding and serve.

SERVES 4–6

TIP
This pudding freezes well for up to three months.

LEMON-SEMOLINA PUDDING

80 g (2¾ oz) semolina
100 g (3½ oz) caster sugar
1 tsp finely grated lemon rind
4 tbsp fresh lemon juice
30 g (1 oz) melted butter
2 large eggs, separated
375 ml (12½ fl oz) milk

1 Sift semolina and add sugar and lemon rind. Add lemon juice, melted butter and egg yolks. Gradually stir milk into sugar mixture and beat until well mixed.

2 Whisk the egg whites until soft peaks form and fold lightly into the lemon batter.

3 Pour into a well-greased medium ovenproof dish. Place the dish in a baking dish or tin of cold water and bake in a preheated oven at 160 °C (325 °F, gas mark 3) for 45–55 minutes. Cover with foil for the last 10 minutes. Serve hot with cream or ice cream.

SERVES 4–6

BUTTERMILK PUDDING

2 large eggs
100 g (3½ oz) caster sugar
15 g (½ oz) butter or margarine, melted
40 g (1¼ oz) plain flour
½ tsp baking powder
pinch of salt
375 ml (12½ fl oz) milk
250 ml (8½ fl oz) buttermilk
1 tsp vanilla essence
grated nutmeg for sprinkling

1 Cream eggs, sugar and butter. Sift flour, baking powder and salt and add. Add milk, buttermilk and essence and mix. Pour into a greased ovenproof dish and sprinkle nutmeg over the top.

2 Bake in a preheated oven at 180 °C (350 °F, gas mark 4) for 45–60 minutes.

SERVES 4

CHOCOLATE FUDGE PUDDING

125 g (4½ oz) plain flour
3 tbsp cocoa powder
2 tsp baking powder
½ tsp salt
140 g (5 oz) caster sugar
30 g (1 oz) butter, melted
250 ml (8½ fl oz) milk
1 large egg
1 tsp vanilla essence

TOPPING
3 tbsp cocoa powder
160 g (5¾ oz) caster sugar
375 ml (12½ fl oz) boiling water

1 Sift together flour, cocoa, baking powder and salt. Add sugar.

2 In another bowl, mix butter, milk, egg and essence and beat into dry ingredients until smooth. Pour into a greased medium ovenproof dish.

3 For topping: sift cocoa and mix with sugar. Sprinkle over dough. Pour boiling water over the top. Bake in a preheated oven at 180 °C (350 °F, gas mark 4) for about 50 minutes.

SERVES 4–6

Clockwise from left: *Chocolate Fudge Pudding, Sticky Date Pudding, Lemon-Semolina Pudding.*

PUMPKIN FRITTERS WITH CARAMEL SAUCE

FRITTERS
60 g (2 oz) plain flour
375 g (13 oz) cooked, mashed pumpkin
2 tsp baking powder
pinch of salt
1 large egg

CARAMEL SAUCE
100 g (3½ oz) granulated sugar
125 ml (4 fl oz) water
125 ml (4 fl oz) milk
1 tsp caramel essence
4 tsp cornflour

1 For fritters: sift the flour and add the remaining ingredients. Mix well. Fry spoonfuls of the batter in shallow oil for a few minutes on each side until golden brown.

2 For sauce: place all ingredients in a heavy-based saucepan. Mix well and boil until sauce thickens. Pour over fritters and serve warm.

MAKES ABOUT 15

CRÊPES WITH CREAMY BANANA AND CARAMEL

CRÊPES
125 g (4½ oz) plain flour
scant ½ tsp salt
2 large eggs
150 ml (5 fl oz) water
about 200 ml (7 fl oz) milk

FILLING
6 bananas, halved lengthways
125 g (4½ oz) butter
200 g (7 oz) soft brown sugar
2 tbsp fresh lemon juice
125 ml (4 fl oz) cream
chopped nuts for topping (optional)

1 For crêpes: sift flour and salt. Whisk eggs with water and milk. Add to dry ingredients and beat to make a thin batter. Leave to stand for 1 hour.

2 Lightly oil a heavy-based frying pan and heat. For each crêpe, pour in just enough batter to cover base and fry until lightly browned on both sides. Keep warm while making filling.

3 For filling: sauté bananas in butter until just soft. Add sugar, lemon juice and cream and cook for 1 minute.

4 Place filling on each crêpe, roll up and spoon over the sauce. Sprinkle with nuts if liked.

MAKES 12–15, DEPENDING ON SIZE OF PAN

VARIATIONS
These crêpes would also be delicious with chocolate or raspberry sauce.
Stack about 6 crêpes on top of each other, layered with banana filling.

TIP
Stack unfilled crêpes between layers of greaseproof paper and freeze.

MALVA PUDDING

50 g (1¾ oz) butter or margarine
100 g (3½ oz) caster sugar
1 large egg
1 tbsp apricot jam
1 tsp vinegar
125 g (4½ oz) plain flour
½ tsp salt
1 tsp bicarbonate of soda
250 ml (8½ fl oz) milk

SAUCE
170 g can evaporated milk
75 g (2½ oz) granulated sugar
1 tsp vanilla essence

1 Cream butter and sugar. Add egg, beating until light and fluffy. Mix in jam and vinegar. Sift dry ingredients and add, with milk, beating until smooth.

2 Spoon into a greased medium ovenproof dish and bake in a preheated oven at 180 °C (350 °F, gas mark 4) for 30–40 minutes.

3 For sauce: heat evaporated milk and sugar until sugar dissolves. Remove from heat and add essence.

4 Pour sauce over the top as soon as the pudding is taken out of the oven.

SERVES 4–6

VARIATION
Substitute evaporated milk with double cream.

Left to right: *Pumpkin Fritters with Caramel Sauce, Malva Pudding.*

103

PEAR AND GINGER ROLY-POLY

BASE
250 g (8½ oz) self-raising flour
scant ½ tsp salt
120 g (4¼ oz) butter or margarine
about 100 ml (3½ fl oz) cold water

FILLING
410 g can pears, drained
and chopped
50 g (1¾ oz) sultanas
½ tsp ground ginger
50 g (1¾ oz) caster sugar

SYRUP
375 ml (12½ fl oz) boiling water
150 g (5½ oz) granulated sugar
30 g (1 oz) butter or margarine

1 For base: sift the flour and salt into a bowl. Rub in butter. Add most of the water and mix to a soft dough. Add more water if necessary.

2 On a lightly floured surface, knead the dough lightly, then roll out to a thickness of about 4 mm (³⁄₈ in) and about 25 x 30 cm (10 x 12 in) in size.

3 For filling: put all the ingredients in a small bowl and mix together until the pears are evenly coated with the ginger and sugar.

4 Spoon the pear mixture evenly over the pastry. Turn up the edges of the dough to hold in the filling and brush dough with water. Roll up like a Swiss roll.

5 Place the roll in a greased, large ovenproof dish.

6 For syrup: mix all the ingredients and pour over roll. Bake in a preheated oven at 180 °C (350 °F, gas mark 4) for 35–45 minutes. Serve with custard.

SERVES 4–6

> ### VARIATION
> Substitute pears with apples and ground ginger with ground cinnamon.

> ### TIP
> Ginger may be fresh, ground or preserved in syrup or sugar. All of these keep for a long time, except fresh root ginger, which will only keep up to two months, provided it's kept in a cool, dry place.

TRADITIONAL CAPE BRANDY PUDDINGS (TIPSY TARTS)

1 tsp bicarbonate of soda
250 ml (8½ fl oz) boiling water
250 g (8½ oz) dried dates, chopped
125 g (4½ oz) butter or margarine
200 g (7 oz) caster sugar
2 large eggs, beaten
185 g (6½ oz) plain flour
scant ½ tsp baking powder
½ tsp salt
35 g (1¼ oz) chopped pecan nuts

SAUCE
60 g (2 oz) butter
150 g (5½ oz) granulated sugar
250 ml (8½ fl oz) water
1 tsp vanilla essence
100 ml (3½ fl oz) brandy

1 Mix the bicarbonate of soda with boiling water and pour it over the chopped dates.

2 Cream the butter and sugar, then beat in the eggs.

3 Sift the flour, baking powder and salt together. Mix the flour and nuts into butter mixture and finally stir in the date mixture.

4 Spoon into greased deep bun tins and bake in a preheated oven at 180 °C (350 °F, gas mark 4) for 15–20 minutes.

5 For sauce: mix the butter, sugar and water and boil until it forms a syrup. Remove from heat and stir in the vanilla essence and brandy. Pour the sauce over the hot puddings and leave to absorb. Serve warm with custard or cream.

SERVES 4–6

> ### VARIATION
> Tipsy tart can be baked in any larger sized dishes for a variation. If using one large dish, bake for 35–40 minutes.

> ### TIP
> These individual brandy puddings can be frozen in airtight containers for up to three months.

Left to right: *Pear and Ginger Roly-poly, Apple and Carrot Pudding.*

APPLE AND CARROT PUDDING

185 g (6½ oz) plain flour
scant ½ tsp salt
1 tsp ground cinnamon
scant ½ tsp ground ginger
½ tsp bicarbonate of soda
1 tsp baking powder
200 g (7 oz) caster sugar
100 g (3½ oz) butter or margarine
2 large eggs
250 ml (8½ fl oz) milk
180 g (6¼ oz) grated apple
180 g (6¼ oz) grated carrots
50 g (1¾ oz) seedless raisins or
chopped pecan nuts
25 g (scant 1 oz) desiccated coconut

LEMON SAUCE
100 g (3½ oz) granulated sugar
4 tbsp water
4 tbsp fresh lemon juice
1 tsp grated lemon rind
15 g (½ oz) butter

1 Sift together flour, salt, cinnamon, ginger, bicarbonate of soda and baking powder. Add the sugar. Rub in the butter with your fingertips.

2 In another bowl, beat the eggs and milk together. Add this mixture to flour mixture, along with apple, carrots, raisins and coconut. Mix well and spoon into a greased, large ovenproof dish.

3 Bake in a preheated oven at 180 °C (350 °F, gas mark 4) for 40 minutes.

4 For sauce: in a saucepan, boil sugar, water, lemon juice and lemon rind together until sugar has dissolved. Add butter and pour sauce over pudding while still hot.

SERVES 4–6

TIP
To keep nuts fresh, store them in the freezer.

CELEBRATIONS

Many of these recipes for special occasions can be prepared in advance, which will leave you with more time on the day.

DARK FRUIT CAKE

250 g (8½ oz) butter or margarine
150 g (5½ oz) brown sugar
5 large eggs
1 tsp vanilla essence
2 tbsp smooth apricot jam
4 tbsp brandy
250 g (8½ oz) plain flour
1 tsp ground ginger
1 tsp mixed spice
1 tsp ground cinnamon
700 g (1½ lb) mixed dried fruit
200 g (7 oz) red glacé cherries,
halved
150 g (5½ oz) whole almonds

1 Cream butter and sugar. Add eggs and beat well until light and fluffy. Add vanilla essence, jam and brandy.

2 Sift flour and spices. Add flour mix, fruit, cherries and nuts to creamed mixture. Mix well until all fruit is coated.

3 Spoon into a well-lined, greased 20 cm (8 in) cake tin. Bake in a preheated oven at 140 °C (275 °F, gas mark 1) for 2½–3 hours. Cool completely in tin before turning out.

MAKES 1 CAKE

TIP
This fruit cake can be baked up to two months before Christmas. Wrap airtight in cling film and foil and store in a cake tin. Spoon 1 tbsp brandy over it weekly.

MARZIPAN (ALMOND PASTE)

500 g (1 lb 2 oz) icing sugar
250 g (8½ oz) ground almonds
½ tsp almond essence
1 large egg yolk (see page 2)
1 tbsp fresh lemon juice
2 tbsp sweet sherry
2 tbsp water
smooth apricot jam

1 Sift icing sugar. Add almonds and almond essence and mix thoroughly.

2 In another bowl, combine egg yolk, lemon juice and sherry and add to almond mixture. Add water if required.

3 Sprinkle icing sugar on work surface and knead mixture to a smooth paste. Add extra sugar if paste is too soft.

4 To cover cake: warm apricot jam and brush over cake. Roll out paste on a surface sprinkled with icing sugar and use a rolling pin to gently place paste over cake.

ROYAL ICING

1 large egg white (see page 2)
400 g (14 oz) icing sugar
1 tsp fresh lemon juice

1 Whisk egg white until foamy. Gradually beat in icing sugar.

2 When mixture reaches soft peak stage, beat in lemon juice. Continue to add icing sugar, whisking until stiff.

SHERRY AND ORANGE CAKE

125 g (4½ oz) butter or margarine
200 g (7 oz) caster sugar
3 large eggs
250 g (8½ oz) plain flour
1 tbsp baking powder
1 tsp grated orange rind
125 ml (4 fl oz) fresh orange juice
4 tbsp sweet sherry

ICING
60 g (2 oz) butter or margarine
325 g (11 oz) icing sugar
1 tsp orange rind
about 80 ml (2¾ fl oz) fresh
orange juice
1 tbsp sweet sherry

1 Cream the butter and sugar together until light and fluffy. Add eggs, beating well after each addition. Sift flour and baking powder together.

2 Mix orange rind and juice with sherry. Add liquid and dry ingredients alternately to the creamed mixture.

3 Pour into two well-greased 20 cm (8 in) cake tins. Bake in a preheated oven at 180 °C (350 °F, gas mark 4) for 20–25 minutes. Cool.

4 For icing: cream butter, add icing sugar and remaining ingredients and beat until smooth and creamy. Use to sandwich and ice the cake.

MAKES 1 LARGE CAKE

Spiral Cake (page 110)

HOT CROSS BUNS

560 g (1¼ lb) white bread flour
1 tsp salt
½ tsp mixed spice
½ tsp ground cinnamon
50 g (1¾ oz) caster sugar
60 g (2 oz) butter or margarine
2 tsp easy-blend yeast
375 ml (12½ fl oz) lukewarm milk
1 large egg, lightly beaten
75 g (2½ oz) sultanas
2 tbsp smooth apricot jam

PASTE FOR CROSSES
60 g (2 oz) plain flour
2 tsp caster sugar
80 ml (2¾ fl oz) water

1 Sift flour, salt and spices. Add sugar and mix. Rub butter into the flour with fingertips. Add yeast.

2 Add milk, egg and sultanas and mix well. Knead on a lightly floured surface until smooth and elastic, cover and leave to rise until doubled in size.

3 Divide dough into 16 pieces and knead each piece into a round shape. Pack buns close together in a greased tin. Set aside in a warm place to prove until doubled in size.

4 For paste: mix all ingredients to a smooth paste. Spoon into a piping bag fitted with a small tube, and pipe crosses onto buns.

5 Bake in a preheated oven at 200 °C (400 °F, gas mark 6) for 20 minutes. Brush tops with hot jam while buns are still hot.

MAKES 16

SPIRAL CAKE

PASTRY BASE
50 g (1¾ oz) butter
1 large egg yolk
2 tsp iced water
½ tsp fresh lemon juice
100 g (3½ oz) plain flour
35 g (1¼ oz) icing sugar
1 tbsp apricot jam

SPONGE
6 large eggs, separated
140 g (5 oz) caster sugar
60 g (2 oz) self-raising flour
25 g (scant 1 oz) cocoa powder
2 tsp instant coffee powder
(optional)

BUTTERCREAM
80 ml (2¾ fl oz) double cream
100 g (3½ oz) white chocolate
125 g (4½ oz) butter
200 g (7 oz) icing sugar
1 tbsp sherry

about 165 g (scant 6 oz) apricot jam
toasted flaked almonds

1 For pastry base: mix butter, egg yolk, iced water and lemon juice.

2 Sift flour and icing sugar and add to mix. Mix until well combined and turn out onto a lightly floured surface. Knead until smooth. Roll out on baking parchment and cut a circle of pastry about 20 cm (8 in) in diameter. Prick with a fork and chill for 15 minutes.

3 Place pastry on a baking tray and bake in a preheated oven at 180 °C for (350 °F, gas mark 4) 10–12 minutes, or until golden. Cool and spread apricot jam on top.

4 For sponge: grease a 24 x 34 cm (9½ x 13½ in) tin. Line the base and sides with greaseproof paper. Beat egg yolks and caster sugar until light and fluffy. Sift flour, cocoa and coffee powder and add to mix, beating well.

5 Whisk egg whites until soft peaks form and fold in with a metal spoon. Spoon mixture into tin.

6 Bake at 180 °C (350 °F, gas mark 4) for 10–12 minutes until light golden brown. Turn out onto a tea towel sprinkled with caster sugar. Remove greaseproof paper and use tea towel to roll from short side. Leave until slightly cooled.

7 For buttercream: heat cream and add chocolate. Mix until smooth and leave to cool. Beat butter, sift icing sugar and add, mixing until well combined. Add sherry and mix well. Gradually beat in the chocolate mixture until thick and creamy.

8 To assemble: unroll cake and cut into strips 6 cm (2½ in) wide. Spread one strip with some jam, then buttercream. Roll up again and place, spiral side up, in the centre of pastry base. Spread jam and buttercream over remaining strips (reserve half of buttercream for topping), and continue spiral until pastry base is covered.

9 Cover and refrigerate for 1 hour. Spread remaining buttercream over the top and decorate with flaked almonds and sifted cocoa powder.

MAKES 1 LARGE CAKE

Left to right: *Hot Cross Buns, Tiramisu Gâteau (page 114).*

PINEAPPLE FRUIT CAKE

440 g can crushed pineapple
500 g (1 lb 2 oz) mixed dried fruit
60 g (2 oz) dried apricots, chopped
100 g (3½ oz) glacé cherries
60 g (2 oz) glacé pineapple (optional)
125 g (4½ oz) dried dates, chopped
125 g (4½ oz) butter or margarine
150 g (5½ oz) brown sugar
125 ml (4 fl oz) sherry
2 large eggs
375 g (13 oz) plain flour
1 tbsp baking powder
scant ½ tsp salt
2 tsp mixed spice

1 Mix all the fruit ingredients in a large, heavy-based saucepan. Add butter and sugar and heat slowly for about 10 minutes, until sugar has dissolved. Remove from heat and add sherry. Leave to cool slightly.

2 Beat eggs and add to fruit mixture. Sift remaining ingredients and add to fruit mixture. Pour into a lined and greased 23 cm (9 in) loaf tin.

3 Bake in a preheated oven at 150 °C (300 °F, gas mark 3) for 1 hour. Reduce the temperature to 140 °C (275 °F, gas mark 1) and bake for 30–40 minutes more. If top starts browning too much, cover with brown paper or foil.

MAKES 1 CAKE

VARIATION
Substitute sherry with port, muscat wine or fruit juice.

BATTENBURG CAKE

180 g (6¼ oz) butter
160 g (5¾ oz) caster sugar
3 large eggs, lightly beaten
250 g (8½ oz) self-raising flour
pinch of salt
scant ½ tsp vanilla essence
scant ½ tsp strawberry essence
a few drops of red food colouring

TOPPING
3 tbsp smooth apricot jam
250 g (8½ oz) almond paste
glacé cherries (optional)

1 Grease and line a 20 cm (8 in) square cake tin. Divide the tin by placing a piece of folded greaseproof paper down the centre.

2 Cream butter and sugar. Add eggs and beat until light and fluffy. Sift flour and salt and add. Divide mixture into two bowls. Add vanilla essence to one bowl and strawberry essence and colouring to the other. Spoon each mixture into its own half of the tin. Bake in a preheated oven at 180 °C (350 °F, gas mark 4) for 25–30 minutes. Turn onto a rack to cool.

3 Trim the cakes and cut each half into two even-sized lengths. Heat jam to soften and sandwich halves together with jam, alternating the colours.

4 Brush jam along outside edges. Roll the almond paste into a rectangle large enough to cover the cake. Wrap paste round the cake and seal the edges. Press edges into a decorative pattern and decorate with cherries.

MAKES 1 CAKE

MINCE PIES

SODA-WATER PASTRY
250 g (8½ oz) plain flour
½ tsp salt
150 g (5½ oz) cold butter
80 ml (2¾ fl oz) iced soda water
1 tbsp fresh lemon juice or brandy

FILLING
454 g jar mincemeat
1 large egg white
caster sugar for sprinkling

1 For pastry: sift flour and salt together. Rub in butter with fingertips until mixture resembles breadcrumbs. Add soda water and lemon juice and mix to a stiff dough.

2 Wrap in cling film and refrigerate for at least 30 minutes. Roll out dough on a floured surface to a thickness of 3 mm (⅛ in). Cut out rounds to line greased tartlet or bun tins.

3 For filling: place heaped teaspoons of mincemeat into each pastry case. Dampen pastry edges with water, cover with another round of pastry and seal.

4 Prick holes in the centre of the lid with a fork or sharp knife and brush with lightly beaten egg white or iced water. Bake in a preheated oven at 200 °C (400 °F, gas mark 6) for about 15 minutes. Sprinkle with caster sugar while still warm.

MAKES ABOUT 24

VARIATION
Substitute pastry lid with crumble or pastry lattice.

Left to right: *Mince Pies, Battenburg Cake, Stollen.*

STOLLEN

280 g (10 oz) white bread flour
½ tsp salt
2 tbsp caster sugar
2 tsp easy-blend yeast
50 g (1¾ oz) butter
1 large egg, beaten
80 ml (2¾ fl oz) warm milk
25 g (scant 1 oz) pecan nuts, chopped
scant ½ tsp grated lemon rind
75 g (2½ oz) mixed dried fruit
30 g (1 oz) glacé cherries
150 g (5½ oz) marzipan (optional)
icing sugar for dusting

1 Sift flour and salt. Add sugar and yeast. Rub in 30 g (1 oz) of butter until mixture resembles fine breadcrumbs. Add egg and milk and mix to a soft dough. If necessary add more milk.

2 Turn onto a floured surface and knead for 10 minutes until dough is smooth and elastic. Place dough in an oiled bowl, cover and leave to rise until doubled in size.

3 Knock back dough, add nuts, rind, fruit and cherries and knead into dough. Roll out on a lightly floured surface into an oval shape of about 15 x 20 cm (6 x 8 in).

4 Knead marzipan until soft. Form a roll to place lengthways in centre of dough. Fold dough over marzipan. Seal edges. Place on a greased baking tray with sealed edge on the bottom. Cover with oiled cling film and leave to rise in a warm place until doubled in size.

5 Melt butter and brush top of bread. Bake in preheated oven at 180 °C (350 °F, gas mark 4) for 35–40 minutes. Cool and dust with icing sugar. Brush with more melted butter and add more icing sugar if liked. Can be stored for 1–2 weeks.

MAKES 1 STOLLEN

SACHERTORTE

*A rich chocolate sponge encased in
rich chocolate icing.*

180 g (6¼ oz) butter or margarine
150 g (5½ oz) caster sugar
6 large eggs, separated
200 g (7 oz) dark chocolate, melted
1 tbsp rum or sherry
1 tsp vanilla essence
125 g (4½ oz) plain flour
5 tbsp smooth apricot jam

ICING
50 ml (3½ tbsp) water
100 g (3½ oz) dark chocolate
50 g (1¾ oz) butter
130 g (4¾ oz) icing sugar

1 Beat butter and sugar until light
and fluffy. Add egg yolks, melted
chocolate, rum and vanilla essence.

2 Whisk egg whites until soft peaks
form. Fold with sifted flour into
creamed mixture.

3 Spoon mixture into a lined and
greased 23 cm (9 in) round springform
tin. Bake in a preheated oven at 180 °C
(350 °F, gas mark 4) for 25–35 minutes.
Turn out onto a wire rack to cool.

4 Cut horizontally into two or three
layers. Spread layers with apricot jam
and stack on top of each other.

5 For icing: heat water, chocolate and
butter in a heavy-based saucepan over
medium heat until melted. Stirring
constantly, remove from heat and stir
in icing sugar. Pour icing over cake,
spread until smooth and leave to set.

MAKES 1 MEDIUM CAKE

VARIATION
Bake in a square tin and cut into
small squares to make petit fours.

TIP
Dip knife in hot water to spread
icing evenly.

TIRAMISU GÂTEAU

round vanilla sponge cake
(see butter cake, page 40)
125 ml (4 fl oz) strong black coffee
80 ml (2¾ fl oz) Tia Maria or sherry
500 g (1 lb 2 oz) sieved cottage
cheese or mascarpone cheese
70 g (2½ oz) caster sugar
250 ml (8½ fl oz) double cream
100 g (3½ oz) chocolate chips
100 g (3½ oz) dark chocolate
icing sugar for dusting

1 Cut the sponge layer horizontally
in half. Use one half to fit the base
of a 20 or 23 cm (8 or 9 in) round,
loose-bottomed cake tin.

2 Mix the coffee with Tia Maria,
and sprinkle half the mixture over
the sponge.

3 Beat the cottage cheese and sugar
together. Whip the cream and fold
it into the cheese mixture. Add the
chocolate chips.

4 Spoon half of cheese mixture over
the cake base.

5 Repeat with second sponge layer,
coffee and cream mixture. Chill
overnight in the refrigerator.

---

6 To serve: remove from tin and
place on a serving plate. Whip more
cream if liked; spread on sides and
pipe on top. Make chocolate curls and
top cake. Dust with icing sugar and
cut into slices.

MAKES 1 LARGE CAKE

TIPS
- Chocolate curls: put chocolate
  in the microwave on medium
  for a few seconds; be careful
  not to melt it. Make curls using
  a potato peeler.
- If preferred, make the sponge in
  advance and freeze.
- Off-cuts or broken pieces can
  also be used. Make sure entire
  tin is covered with the sponge.

CHRISTMAS ALMOND BISCUITS

250 g (8½ oz) butter
105 g (3¾ oz) caster sugar
1 tsp vanilla essence
250 g (8½ oz) plain flour
150 g (5½ oz) nibbed almonds
icing sugar for rolling

1 Cream butter and sugar. Add
vanilla essence and sifted flour. Add
almonds and roll into small balls. Place
on a greased baking tray and press
them lightly with a fork.

2 Bake in a preheated oven at
200 °C (400 °F, gas mark 6) for
10–12 minutes. Roll warm biscuits in
icing sugar and cool on a wire rack.

MAKES ABOUT 30

Left to right: *Sachertorte, Christmas Shape Biscuits, Christmas Almond Biscuits.*

CHRISTMAS SHAPE BISCUITS

125 g (4½ oz) butter or margarine
52 g (2 oz) caster sugar
½ tsp vanilla essence
185 g (6½ oz) plain flour
scant ½ tsp salt
1 tbsp milk

GLACÉ ICING

130 g (4¾ oz) icing sugar
about 2 tbsp boiling water
scant ½ tsp vanilla essence
a few drops of food colouring

1 Cream butter and sugar together. Add vanilla essence.

2 Sift flour and salt, add to creamed mixture and knead to form a stiff dough. Add milk if needed. Roll out to a thickness of 4 mm (¼ in) and, using a Christmas biscuit cutter, cut out shapes. If hanging the biscuits from a tree, make a hole in the dough.

3 Place on a greased baking tray and bake in a preheated oven at 180 °C (350 °F, gas mark 4) for 10–15 minutes, or until light brown on the edges.

4 Remove biscuits from tray using a pallette knife. Place on a rack to cool.

5 For icing: sift the icing sugar and add enough water to make a smooth consistency. Add the vanilla essence and colouring of choice.

6 Ice cooled biscuits and decorate with hundreds and thousands, silver balls and chocolate vermicelli. The biscuits may also be dipped into melted chocolate before decorating.

MAKES ABOUT 30

KIDS

Spending time making biscuits, puddings or any other creative activities should be a magical experience for children. It is important that they learn to use their own initiative and imagination to change things. The section on party cakes should involve the children – do not always leave the cake as a surprise. Basic techniques, such as sifting the ingredients, should be taught so that they have a perception of baking and grow up being able to do something for themselves in the kitchen.

ROCKY ROAD COOKIES

125 g (4½ oz) butter
100 g (3½ oz) light brown sugar
2 large eggs
185 g (6½ oz) plain flour
2 tbsp cocoa powder
scant ½ tsp salt

TOPPING
60 g (2 oz) marshmallows, chopped
80 g (2¾ oz) milk chocolate, chopped, or chocolate chips

1 Cream butter and sugar. Add eggs and beat until light and fluffy.

2 Sift flour, cocoa and salt and add to mixture, stirring until well combined. Drop spoonfuls of mixture onto a greased baking tray. Bake in a preheated oven at 180 °C (350 °F, gas mark 4) for about 8 minutes. Remove from oven.

3 For topping: sprinkle with marshmallows and chocolate chunks, pressing slightly into cookies. Return to oven for a further 2–3 minutes to melt slightly. Cool on wire racks.

MAKES ABOUT 28

TIP
When cutting marshmallows, use scissors regularly dipped in flour to prevent sticking.

PEANUT BUTTER COOKIES

60 g (2 oz) butter or margarine
65 g (2¼ oz) smooth or crunchy peanut butter
100 g (3½ oz) brown sugar
100 g (3½ oz) caster sugar
1 large egg
125 g (4½ oz) plain flour
scant ½ tsp salt
1 tsp bicarbonate of soda

1 Cream the butter and peanut butter until soft. Add sugars gradually, beating well.

2 Add egg and beat until light and fluffy. Sift together flour, salt and bicarbonate of soda and add to mixture. Mix well.

3 Shape teaspoonfuls of the mixture into balls and place on lightly greased baking trays. Bake in a preheated oven at 180 °C (350 °F, gas mark 4) for 8–10 minutes. Turn out onto a wire rack to cool. Store in an airtight container.

MAKES ABOUT 30

VARIATION
Serve these cookies crumbled over vanilla ice cream for a delicious variation.

CRUMPETS

2 large eggs
50 g (1¾ oz) caster sugar
125 g (4½ oz) plain flour
1½ tsp baking powder
scant ½ tsp salt
125 ml (4 fl oz) milk
30 g (1 oz) butter or margarine, melted
sunflower oil for frying

1 Beat eggs and sugar together until light and fluffy.

2 Sift flour, baking powder and salt and add to egg mixture. Add milk and melted butter and mix well.

3 Place spoonfuls of batter in a heated frying pan and shallow-fry until light brown on both sides. Serve with butter and grated Cheddar cheese.

MAKES 15–20

VARIATION
Add four mashed bananas for banana crumpets.

TIP
Crumpets are best eaten on the day they were made, but they can be frozen for up to two months.

Rocky Road Cookies

BASIC SPONGE FOR NOVELTY CAKES

A variety of novelty cake tins is available in specialised kitchen shops. Alternatively, bake a basic sponge and then cut it into the desired shape.

HOT MILK SPONGE CAKE
4 large eggs
260 g (8¾ oz) caster sugar
250 g (8½ oz) plain flour
1 tbsp baking powder
250 ml (8½ fl oz) milk
100 g (3½ oz) butter or margarine
1 tsp vanilla essence

BASIC ICING
100 g (3½ oz) soft butter
250 g (8½ oz) icing sugar
1 tsp vanilla essence
about 2 tbsp milk
food colouring of choice

CHOCOLATE ICING
100 g (3½ oz) soft butter
250 g (8½ oz) icing sugar
2 tbsp cocoa powder
2 tbsp hot water
scant ½ tsp vanilla essence
about 2 tbsp milk

1 For sponge: Cream eggs and sugar together until thick and light.

2 Sift the flour and baking powder together and fold into the egg and sugar mixture.

3 In a saucepan, heat the milk and butter. Do not boil. Stir milk mixture and vanilla essence into batter. Spoon into two greased 20 cm (8 in) round cake tins. Bake in a preheated oven at 180 °C (350 °F, gas mark 4) for 25–30 minutes.

4 For both icings: beat all the ingredients until smooth and creamy.

5 Decorate with sweets, taking colour and size into consideration. You can use silver balls, hundreds and thousands, chocolate chips, vermicelli, liquorice or fruited gum sweets.

MAKES 2 SPONGES

VARIATION
Chocolate cake: Add 3½ tbsp cocoa powder to dry ingredients. For other flavours, add 1 tsp essence to basic sponge and a few drops of food colouring.

TIP
The basic sponge can be doubled for baking in a large cake tin.

PEANUT AND RAISIN SQUARES

150 g (5½ oz) butter or margarine
100 g (3½ oz) caster sugar
75 g (2½ oz) seedless raisins
75 g (2½ oz) peanuts
40 g (1¼ oz) desiccated coconut
125 g (4½ oz) plain flour

1 Melt butter in a heavy-based saucepan. Add remaining ingredients and mix well. Press into a greased 16 x 26 cm (6½ x 10½ in) tray bake tin.

2 Bake in a preheated oven at 180 °C (350 °F, gas mark 4) for 20 minutes. Cool completely, then cut into squares.

MAKES ABOUT 18

VANILLA CUP CAKES

125 g (4½ oz) butter or margarine
150 g (5½ oz) caster sugar
3 large eggs
1 tsp vanilla essence
250 g (8½ oz) plain flour
1 tbsp baking powder
scant ½ tsp salt
125 ml (4 fl oz) milk

1 Beat butter and sugar together. Add eggs and beat until light and creamy. Add vanilla essence.

2 Sift flour, baking powder and salt and add, with milk, to egg mixture. Mix well. Fill paper liners in bun tins to two-thirds full.

3 Bake in a preheated oven at 180 °C (350 °F, gas mark 4) for 12–15 minutes.

MAKES ABOUT 24

VARIATIONS
Substitute vanilla essence with any other flavour, such as lemon or strawberry, and add a few drops of food colouring.
To make fairy cakes: cut a thin slice from the top of each cup cake and cut it in half. Whip double cream with a little caster sugar until stiff. Spoon cream on top of cut surface and place cut tops on cream to resemble wings. Dust with icing sugar.

Novelty Cakes

COCONUT ICE SLICES

PASTRY
50 g (1¾ oz) butter or margarine
2 tbsp caster sugar
½ tsp vanilla essence
1 large egg yolk
60 g (2 oz) plain flour
2 tbsp cornflour

FILLING
160 g (5¾ oz) desiccated coconut
200 g (7 oz) caster sugar
2 large eggs
60 g (2 oz) glacé cherries, chopped

ICING
130 g (4¾ oz) icing sugar
1 tbsp milk
15 g (½ oz) butter, melted

1 For pastry: beat butter, sugar and vanilla essence until creamy. Add egg yolk and beat well. Fold in sifted flour and cornflour and press into a greased 16 x 26 cm (6½ x 10½ in) tray bake tin.

2 For filling: combine coconut, sugar and eggs in a bowl. Add cherries and mix well. Spoon filling evenly over pastry.

3 Bake in a preheated oven at 180 °C (350 °F, gas mark 4) for 25–30 minutes. Cool in tin.

4 For icing: sift icing sugar and add milk and melted butter. Mix until smooth and spread over the cooled cake. Cut into slices.

MAKES ABOUT 28

FRUITY CHOCOLATE BISCUITS

250 g (8½ oz) butter or margarine
210 g (7½ oz) caster sugar
2 large eggs
1 tsp vanilla essence
250 g (8½ oz) self-raising flour
½ tsp salt
300 g (10½ oz) mixed dried fruit
125 g (4½ oz) dark chocolate, coarsely chopped
200 g (7 oz) cornflakes

1 Cream butter and sugar. Add eggs and vanilla essence and beat until light and fluffy.

2 Sift flour and salt and add to egg mixture. Add dried fruit, chocolate and half the cornflakes.

3 Crush rest of cornflakes and roll teaspoonfuls of mixture in cornflakes. Place on a greased baking tray.

4 Bake in a preheated oven at 180 °C (350 °F, gas mark 4) for 15 minutes, or until light brown.

MAKES ABOUT 70

VARIATION
Substitute chocolate pieces with chocolate chips.

TIP
These biscuits are very crumbly. Make sure you work very carefully to prevent breakage.

BANANA-OAT SQUARES

125 g (4½ oz) butter
65 g (2¼ oz) light brown sugar
125 g (4½ oz) golden syrup
240 g (8 oz) rolled oats
60 g (2 oz) plain flour
½ tsp ground cinnamon
scant ½ tsp ground ginger
½ tsp baking powder
pinch of salt
3 bananas, mashed

1 Melt butter, sugar and syrup over low heat. Stir in oats. Sift flour, spices, baking powder and salt and add to mixture. Stir well.

2 Add bananas and mix. Turn into a greased 16 x 26 cm (6½ x 10½ in) tray bake tin. Bake in a preheated oven at 180 °C (350 °F, gas mark 4) for 20–25 minutes. Cut into squares.

MAKES ABOUT 24

PLAY DOUGH

250 g (8½ oz) plain flour
500 ml (17 fl oz) water
140 g (5 oz) salt
1 tbsp cream of tartar
1 tbsp sunflower oil
¾–1 tsp food colouring of choice

1 Mix all ingredients, except colouring, in a heavy-based saucepan. Stir over medium heat until it forms a ball.

2 Cool and knead well. Add colouring and knead again. Store in an airtight container to prevent drying out.

MAKES 800 G (1¾ LB)

Clockwise from left: *Fruity Chocolate Biscuits, Banana-Oat Squares, Coconut Ice Slices.*

CHEESE AND HERB PUFFS

125 g (4½ oz) self-raising flour
1 tsp baking powder
pinch of salt
scant ½ tsp mustard powder
2 tsp chopped fresh parsley
or ½ tsp dried
100 g (3½ oz) grated Cheddar cheese
1 large egg
125 ml (4 fl oz) milk
15 g (½ oz) butter, melted

1 Sift together flour, baking powder, salt and mustard powder. Add parsley and cheese.

2 In another bowl, whisk egg, milk and melted butter.

3 Add wet mixture to dry ingredients and mix until just combined.

4 Spoon into greased bun tins and bake in a preheated oven at 200 °C (400 °F, gas mark 6) for 10–12 minutes. Serve warm.

MAKES ABOUT 12 LARGE OR 24 MINI

VARIATION
Substitute parsley with any other herbs of choice.

GINGERBREAD MEN

125 g (4½ oz) butter
70 g (2½ oz) caster sugar
65 g (2¼ oz) golden syrup
315 g (10¾ oz) plain flour
1 tsp ground ginger
½ tsp ground cinnamon
2 tsp bicarbonate of soda
1 large egg

ICING
230 g (8 oz) icing sugar
1 tbsp orange juice

1 Place butter, sugar and syrup in a heavy-based saucepan. Bring to the boil over moderate heat until sugar has dissolved. Leave to cool.

2 Sift flour, spices and bicarbonate of soda and add to syrup mix. Add egg and beat well. Mix further, using your hands, to form a stiff dough.

3 Roll out dough until about 6 mm (¼ in) in thickness. Cut out gingerbread men shapes and place on greased baking trays. Bake in preheated oven at 180 °C (350 °F, gas mark 4) for about 10 minutes until light brown.

4 Place on a wire rack to cool.

5 For icing: sift icing sugar and add enough orange juice to make a stiff icing. Put into a piping bag and ice.

MAKES ABOUT 15

VARIATION
Decorate with currants, chocolate chips or cherries before baking.

COCONUT JAM SQUARES

250 g (8½ oz) plain flour
2 tsp baking powder
pinch of salt
100 g (3½ oz) caster sugar
100 g (3½ oz) butter or margarine
1 large egg
4 tbsp milk
165 g (5¾ oz) smooth apricot jam

TOPPING
1 large egg
100 g (3½ oz) caster sugar
120 g (4¼ oz) desiccated coconut
2 tbsp milk
1 tsp vanilla essence

1 Sift flour, baking powder, salt and sugar. Rub in butter.

2 Beat egg and add milk. Mix into dry ingredients. Press into a greased 23 x 32 cm (9 x 13 in) Swiss roll tin. Spread with jam.

3 For topping: beat egg, add sugar and beat again. Add the remaining ingredients. Spread on top of jam. Bake in a preheated oven at 200 °C (400 °F, gas mark 6) for 15–20 minutes. Cut into squares while still warm.

MAKES ABOUT 30

Left to right: *Cheese and Herb Puffs, Coconut Jam Squares, Gumdrop Cookies.*

GUMDROP COOKIES

200 g (7 oz) butter, softened
150 g (5½ oz) caster sugar
1 tsp vanilla essence
1 large egg
155 g (5½ oz) plain flour
½ tsp baking powder
½ tsp bicarbonate of soda
scant ½ tsp salt
80 g (2¾ oz) rolled oats
125 g (4½ oz) gumdrops, chopped

1 Cream the butter, sugar and vanilla essence. Add the egg and beat until light and fluffy.

2 Sift the flour, baking powder, bicarbonate of soda and salt. Add to the egg mixture. Add the oats and gumdrops and mix well.

3 Drop heaped teaspoonfuls onto a greased baking tray, leaving enough space for spreading.

4 Bake in a preheated oven at 180 °C (350 °F, gas mark 4) for 10–12 minutes. Cool on wire racks.

MAKES ABOUT 30

TIP
To cut gumdrops easily, use kitchen scissors dipped in cold water.

GENERAL MISTAKES AND CAUSES

CAKES

Cake has risen unevenly in oven.
- Flour not blended sufficiently into main mixture.
- Oven temperature too high.
- Side of tin unevenly greased.

Cake sinks in centre.
- Too much sugar.
- Batter too dry.
- Under-manipulation (mixing).
- Tin too small.
- Oven temperature too low.
- Cake not baked through.
- Oven door opened during baking.
- Too much raising agent.
- Too much liquid.
- Batter left too long before baking.

Cake rises and sinks in oven.
- Too much liquid.
- Too much raising agent.
- Oven opened too soon or too often.

Small brown speckles on surface of cake or biscuits.
- Granulated sugar used instead of caster sugar.

Cake texture heavy.
- Butter, sugar and eggs not beaten together long enough.
- Flour stirred in too vigorously.
- Too much flour added to creamed mixture.
- Oven temperature too low.

Coarse, grainy texture.
- Too much raising agent.
- Insufficient creaming.
- Too much fat.

Dry and crumbly texture.
- Baked too long at low temperature.
- Too much raising agent.

Tunnels and large holes.
- Ingredients over-mixed.
- Oven temperature too high.

A dense and heavy cake texture.
- Not enough air whisked into egg and sugar mixture.
- Flour not folded in gently enough.
- Oven temperature too low.

Sunken fruit mixture.
- Fruit wet or damp.
- Mixture too soft to support weight of fruit.

Cracked top crust.
- Mixture too stiff.
- Initial oven temperature too high.

Overly browned crust.
- Too much sugar.
- Oven temperature too high.

Bitter or soapy after-taste.
- Too much baking powder/ bicarbonate of soda.

MUFFINS

Muffins unevenly shaped.
- Batter uneven in tins.
- Batter too runny.
- Batter not mixed enough.

Muffins peak too high in centre.
- Over-mixed batter.
- Too much flour.
- Too much baking powder.

Muffins fell flat when taken out of oven.
- Too little baking powder.
- Too much fat or sugar.
- Batter too thin.
- Pans too small.

Muffins with tunnels.
- Mixed for too long.
- Used an electric mixer.
- Too much baking powder.
- Oven temperature too high.

PASTRIES

Rolled out pastries

Pastry shrinks away from sides of the flan tin during baking.
- Pastry stretched while being rolled out.
- Pastry not rested before and after being rolled.

Pastry hard and tough.
- Pastry over-mixed in bowl or kneaded too much.
- Too much liquid added to rubbed-in flour and butter mixture.
- Too much flour used for dusting work surface when rolling out pastry.

Choux pastry

Pastry collapsed when removed from oven.
- Pastry not baked for long enough.
- Hole not pierced through base of cooked pastry. Trapped steam caused pastry to go soft again.
- Oven temperature too high.

BISCUITS

Biscuits lose shape during baking.
- Too much liquid.
- Dough not cool before baking.

Too soft.
- Not stored airtight.
- More than one type of biscuit stored in container.

BREADS

Heavy bread.
- Dough too stiff or soft.
- Underproofed.
- Underbaked.

Coarse texture.
- Under-kneading.
- Overproofed.
- Dough too soft.
- Oven temperature too low.

Small volume.
- Too much sugar or.fat.
- Underproofed.
- Flour with poor gluten content.

Uneven shape.
- Bad shaping.
- Pan too small for amount of dough.
- Over- or underproofed.
- Pans too close together in oven.

Cracked crust.
- Dough too stiff.
- Underproofed.
- Oven too hot.

CORRECTING CAKE FLAWS
Use some of the following ideas:

Petit Fours
Cut cake in 3 cm (1¼ in) squares and sandwich together with apricot jam. Pour over glacé icing and decorate.

Tray bakes
Cut into squares, dip in chocolate icing and roll in desiccated coconut, chocolate vermicelli or chopped nuts.

Trifle
Use any offcuts for trifle. Fresh crumbs can also be used for trifle or any steamed puddings.

Gâteau
Cut cake horizontally into three or four layers. Pour sherry, Port or brandy over and layer with custard, whipped cream or any other fillings of choice. Decorate the cake with cream, chocolate and any fruit of choice.

Ring cake
When a cake has sunk in the centre, cut the centre out and make a ring cake. Fill the ring with fresh fruit and ice and decorate the cake.

GLOSSARY

ALMOND PASTE A mixture of two-thirds sugar and one-third ground almonds combined with syrup or enough eggs to make a paste.

BAKING BLIND Baking a pastry case without a filling. The pastry is pricked all over with a fork, covered with greaseproof paper and topped with dried beans (to retain the shape of the pastry during baking). It is baked for 5–10 minutes and then the beans and paper are removed.

BAKING POWDER A mixture containing bicarbonate of soda, starch and acids, used to make cakes and some light dough rise. The acids react with the bicarbonate of soda when liquid is added, releasing the carbon dioxide that aerates the mixture.

BEAT To incorporate air into an ingredient or mixture by agitating it vigorously with a spoon, fork, whisk or electric mixer.

BICARBONATE OF SODA Sodium bicarbonate, an alkali that reacts with acids (such as buttermilk, yoghurt or cream of tartar) and releases carbon dioxide, which aerates the mixture.

BLANCH To immerse food briefly in boiling water to soften it (for example, vegetables), skin it (such as nuts), get rid of excess salt, or kill enzymes before freezing.

BLEND To fold or mix two or more ingredients together with a spoon, fork, whisk or electric mixer.

BOUQUET GARNI Small bunch of herbs (often consisting of thyme, marjoram, parsley and a bay leaf) tied together with string or placed in a small muslin bag. Used to flavour soups and stews.

BRAN The outer layer or husk of the cereal grain; a major source of fibre.

CARAMELISE To heat sugar or syrup slowly until brown in colour (forms caramel).

CONSISTENCY The texture of a mixture, for example firm, dropping or soft.

CREAM OF TARTAR Leavening acid with a rapid action to produce carbon dioxide. Used as the acid ingredient in some baking powders. It is added to candy and frosting mixtures for a creamier consistency, and to egg whites (such as meringue) before whisking to improve stability and volume and for a whiter colour.

CRÊPE A thin, light pancake.

CRYSTALLISATION When sugar that has been dissolved in a liquid forms crystals.

CURDLE To cause fresh milk, a sauce or other liquid to separate into solids and liquids by overheating or by adding acid (such as lemon juice or vinegar), or to cause creamed butter and sugar to separate by adding the eggs too rapidly.

DROPPING CONSISTENCY The required texture of a cake or pudding mixture just before cooking. Test for it by taking a spoonful of the mixture and holding the spoon on its side above the bowl.

DUMPLINGS Small balls of dough, stuffing or vegetable mixture, which are steamed or poached. They are used in puddings and to garnish soups and stews.

DUST To sprinkle flour on a working surface or inside a tin to prevent dough from sticking. Also to sprinkle lightly with flour, cornflour, icing sugar and so on.

ÉCLAIR A long, hollow, finger-shaped puff made from choux pastry, filled with cream and topped with melted chocolate.

EGG WASH To brush on a mixture of fresh egg and water to put a shine on the crusts of breads and rolls.

ESSENCE Used for flavouring puddings and confectionery, made from natural or synthetic ingredients, or blends of both.

FLAN Pastry case baked in a flan tin, traditionally with a sweet or savoury custard filling. May also be a custard pudding like crème caramel.

FOLDING IN Combining a whisked or creamed mixture with other ingredients by cutting and folding so that it retains its lightness. A large metal spoon is used.

FRY To cook in fat or oil, either deep or shallow.

GATEAU A rich, decorated cake, often layered, which may include liqueur, cream, nuts and fruit.

GELATINE Animal-derived gelling agent sold in powdered form or as leaf gelatine.

GLAZE To brush on a liquid to improve appearance and, sometimes, flavour. Ingredients for glazes include beaten egg, egg white, milk, syrup and melted jam.

GLUTEN The insoluble wheat protein left after hydration. This elastic substance assists in trapping carbon dioxide in bread dough. The strength of a flour's gluten determines its use. Bread dough requires a high gluten flour, while a cake mixture requires a low gluten, softer flour.

GREASING To apply a thin coating of fat or oil inside a cake, bread or pie tin to prevent sticking.

ICING The sweet coating on a cake or other baked item.

INCORPORATING The act of mixing ingredients together in a recipe.

KNEAD To work ingredients into a mass of bread dough by mixing, usually by hand.

KNOCK BACK The process of deflating a dough that has risen to ensure an even texture.

MARZIPAN A confection, made from almond paste, sugar and egg whites, used for modelling fruits, figures and so on.

MERINGUE Usually made by whisking egg whites with sugar. It is used for a topping or making shells and biscuits.

MIXING Blending ingredients into a mass.

MIXING TIME This has a direct effect on leavening. Yeast, baking powder and bicarbonate of soda cannot do their jobs if the mixing time is incorrect. If dough or batter is over-mixed and gets too hot, carbon dioxide will escape before the mixture is baked. Under-mixing may cause uneven disbursement and dense grain, holes and lack of volume.

MOLASSES A by-product of cane or beet sugar refinement.

PETIT FOURS Tiny sponge cakes that have been iced and decorated.

PIPING BAG A bag fitted with a tube which is used to pipe whipped cream, meringue, icing, savoury butter or other pastes into neat, decorative shapes.

PROVE To leave bread dough to rise after shaping.

PURÉE Any fruit or vegetable rubbed through a sieve or worked in a blender or food processor until smooth.

REDUCE To thicken a sauce or other liquid by boiling rapidly in an open pan.

RIND The outer layer of citrus fruits that is finely grated to use as flavouring.

RUB IN Incorporating fat into flour when a short texture is required. Used for pastry, cakes, scones and biscuits. Rub with the fingertips to give a crumbly texture.

SAUTÉ Lightly pan-fried in a small amount of oil or butter until golden.

SIFT To shake dry ingredients through a sieve to remove lumps, to aerate and to mix.

SIMMER To cook in liquid that is just below boiling point.

SOUFFLÉ A puffed up sweet or savoury dish, made light by adding stiffly whisked egg white (can be baked or steamed).

VOL-AU-VENT A light, flaky case of puff pastry with a lid, filled with a sweet or savoury mixture.

INDEX

Page numbers in *italics* refer to photographs.